WITNEY

A History

The western channel of the River Windrush, as depicted on a postcard c.1912.
Cogges Church can be glimpsed to the left of the picture.

WITNEY
A History

Stanley C. Jenkins

PHILLIMORE

2010

Published by

PHILLIMORE and CO. LTD

Andover, Hampshire, England

www.phillimore.co.uk

ISBN 978-1-86077-620-5

Printed and bound in Malta

Manufacturing managed by

Jellyfish Print Solutions Ltd

Contents

List of Illustrations

Frontispiece: *The western channel of the River Windrush.*

Introduction

Witney grew up as a result of a policy of deliberate planning and development carried out by successive Bishops of Winchester, and by the end of the Middle Ages the town had become a busy marketing centre with a thriving textile industry. The local population tended to be pro-Parliament during the Civil War and when, at the Restoration, the more extreme Puritans excluded themselves from the Church of England Witney became a centre of nonconformity, with strong Quaker, Baptist and Independent congregations. In the 18th century John Wesley paid many visits to the area, and Methodism eventually became the dominant form of local Dissent. Meanwhile, aided by the Protestant values of thrift, sobriety and hard work, the blanket trade had gone from strength to strength and by 1800 there were five textile mills in and around the town.

In 1858 the leading townsfolk joined forces with local landowners to build the Witney Railway and as a result large quantities of cheap coal could be brought into the town. This in turn facilitated the introduction of steam-powered mills such as Bridge Street Mill in the 1860s and Mount Mill in 1901. By 1914 there were six mills in operation, divided between four main blanket-making firms, while in 1933 the Yorkshire firm of James Walker and Son of Mirfield opened a further mill – bringing new employment to Witney when other areas were suffering from the effects of the Great Depression.

In 1951 Witney, which then had a population of about 5,300, became a centre of light engineering when Smiths Industries established a large factory on a former aerodrome to the west of the town. The presence of Smiths and other industrial concerns ensured that by the 1950s Witney was no longer entirely dependent upon the woollen industry, although the town remained famous as a centre of the blanket-manufacturing industry until the closure of Witney Mill on 19 July 2002. Despite the loss of its once famous industry, the town's population continued to grow, from *c.*10,800 in the 1960s to 22,765 at the time of the 2001 census.

1

Origins and Early History

Witney is a small town in West Oxfordshire. It is situated at the point where the old high road from London to Milford Haven crosses the River Windrush and was once famous as a centre of the West England textile industry, the principal products being blankets and other heavy broadcloths. Despite its long industrial history, Witney has never looked like an 'industrial' centre, the mills which produced its staple products being surprisingly unobtrusive, while the town has even today retained much of its essentially 'Cotswold' character – the predominant building material being grey oolitic limestone.

The scenery in the West Oxfordshire area is dictated by the underlying geology, which generally speaking consists of a plateau of oolitic limestone, with a belt of low-lying Oxford Clay bordering the River Thames to the south. The oolitic uplands which give the area its distinctive Cotswold character reach a maximum elevation of 810ft above mean sea level in the vicinity of Chipping Norton, though the hills fall gradually towards the south, where they eventually meet the Oxford claylands. These claylands are not entirely flat because they are dotted with 'islands' of cornbrash, upon which many of the settlements are built; Witney is sited on a low island or hillock in what was formerly a marshy area between two divergent channels of the River Windrush.

Early Settlement

In prehistoric times the area around present-day Witney was covered by a dense forest, parts of which would, in later years, become the Royal Forest of Wychwood. The earliest inhabitants of the district were able to penetrate this great forest by means of the river valleys, though the relative paucity of prehistoric sites in the area suggests that the district was sparsely settled – early man preferred the open downland on the south side of the River Thames in what is now Berkshire and Wiltshire.

The first archaeological evidence of settlement within the wooded areas comes from the Neolithic period (*c*.3000-2400 B.C.). Large quantities of flint implements, including scrapers, boring tools, knives and axe fragments, as well as arrow heads and waste flakes, have been discovered in a cluster of sites near the village of Minster Lovell, to the west of Witney, indicating the presence of one or more permanent or semi-permanent settlements some four thousand years ago.

Archaeological evidence from the Bronze Age (*c*.2400-1500 B.C.) and the Iron Age (*c*. 1500 B.C.-A.D. 410) suggests there were settlements in the forested area to the north of present-day Witney and, more especially, in the lower-lying district south of the town. Round barrows and other Bronze-Age features have been identified around Crawley and Leafield, while the gravel terraces around Standlake and Stanton Harcourt have yielded a wealth of archaeological material. Witney itself has produced very few early finds, the most significant object found within its boundaries being a Bronze-Age sword, which was discovered, broken into two pieces, in the stream known as 'Emma's Dyke', to the south-west of Corn Street.

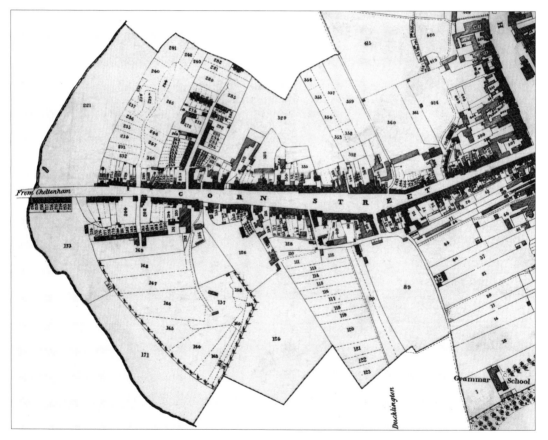

1 *Corn Street, as depicted on the Witney Tithe Map of 1839-40, showing the widening of the street which is thought to be a legacy of the original village settlement on Witta's Island. Emma's Dyke can be seen to the left, while the curious bend at the eastern end of the street may mark the physical join between the original village and the Bishop's new town.*

In the Iron Age, the indigenous Celtic and pre-Celtic people of the district were known as the Dobunni, while their neighbours to the south were the Atrebates. One or two late Iron-Age coins have been found in the Witney area, including a Dubunnic gold coin inscribed with the name of 'Bodvoc', and a silver coin of Epaticcus, who ruled the Atrebates around A.D. 30. These early Britons were primarily farmers with a preference for settlement on the gravel terraces alongside the Thames – a great untamed river which they probably called the Tam-ouse, or 'Broad Water'.

An alternative means of access to the forested areas was afforded by the existence of natural 'ridge way' routes, one of which extended westwards across what is now West Oxfordshire between Long Hanborough, Witney and Burford. It was comparatively easy for travellers to find their way along these routes, even when trees or undergrowth formed impediments to movement. In wintertime the ridge ways did not become impassable as a result of flooding while, during the summer months, they enabled early man to move livestock to temporary summer pastures.

The Romano-British Period

In A.D. 43 the Emperor Claudius ordered the invasion of Britain and dispatched four Roman legions across the Channel, the well-trained heavy infantrymen of these regular legions being supported by a similar number of auxiliaries, including Gallic and Thracian units. Although the Roman invaders met initial resistance in the Medway area, and along the line of the lower Thames, the Dobunni appear to have welcomed Roman rule and there was, in consequence, no conflict between the Roman army and the indigenous Britons in the Upper Thames Valley.

The period of Roman occupation was significant in that it saw the construction of Akeman Street, a major artery of communication cutting through Wychwood Forest from north-east to south-west, which facilitated the creation of a network of subsidiary tracks into the woodland. Akeman Street itself was a properly surfaced highway, though most of the connecting roads were little more than woodland tracks. Nevertheless, this new infrastructure enabled the Romans and romanised Britons to create a system of large estates within the forested area, and thus, at the dawn of the first millennium, the systematic settlement of West Oxfordshire commenced.

As far as can be ascertained there were no large towns in the Witney area during the Roman period, the nearest towns being at *Alchester* (Bicester), some 20 miles to the east, and *Corinium* (Cirencester), about 29 miles to the west. The Roman countryside was covered by a patchwork of country estates, each of which had a large house or villa at its centre. These villas were typically situated in convenient proximity of Akeman Street, good communications being an essential prerequisite for large-scale commercial agriculture. One of the best-known villas was that at East End, near North Leigh, though there were several others in the area, including Shakenoak Villa near New Yatt. The manor of Witney probably evolved from one of these Romano-British estates, though the original village settlement did not appear until much later.

The Anglo-Saxon Period

The end of Roman rule in A.D. 410 was followed by a period of turmoil known as the Dark Ages in which urban life was abandoned and the Upper Thames Valley was colonised by settlers from Europe such as the Saxons. The number of invaders must have been relatively small, but the newcomers were able to settle among the Britons and impose their Germanic language and customs upon the earlier Celtic population.

The existing Romano-British inhabitants of the district may have been killed or driven away, but archaeological discoveries hint that Celtic communities may have continued to exist throughout the period of the Saxon 'invasions', while occupation continued at Roman sites such as Shakenoak Villa. Excavations at Dark-Age burial sites have produced a mixture of Romano-British and Saxon artefacts – suggesting that the Britons may have married and intermingled with the Anglo-Saxon settlers to produce a mixed Anglo-Celtic population.

The West Saxon royal family believed that their Germanic ancestors had fought several major battles during the sixth century, one of these being in the year 571, when a warrior named Cuthwulf captured Aylesbury, Benson, Limbury and Eynsham from the Britons and thereby began the long process of absorbing the Romano-Britons of the Upper Thames Valley into the Kingdom of Wessex. It suited later West Saxon propandists to believe that sixth-century Saxons such as Cuthwulf were 'kings' or 'princes', although Bede, writing in the eighth century, referred to them as the 'Gewise', a difficult word to translate but one which implies they were a gang of mercenaries known as 'The Trusties' who had seized control of the Upper Thames Valley and were offering military protection to the local inhabitants.

The 'Gewise' fought many further battles throughout the sixth century, one of these engagements being at Stoke Lyne in North Oxfordshire where, according to the *Anglo-Saxon Chronicle*, 'Ceawlin and Cutha fought against the Britons' and Cutha was killed, although the Saxons were ultimately successful and 'Ceawlin captured many vills, and countless spoils, and went away in anger to his own land'. The number of warriors involved in these clashes is likely to have been very small, but the cumulative effects of numerous small skirmishes was significant in that, by some process that we do not fully understand, the 'Gewise' became petty kings and their territory in and around the Upper Thames Valley became the nucleus of the Kingdom of Wessex.

The Origins of Witney

We know little about military or political organisation during the Dark Ages, though it seems likely that society would have been organised as a tribal heirarchy, with each community owing allegiance to a local chieftain or warlord. Meanwhile, the collapse of centralised authority meant that people congregated together for mutual protection, perhaps in ethnic or family groups. In this way villages and hamlets were formed, some of which, such as Witney, being in secluded and heavily forested areas to guarantee a modicum of security in harsh and troubled times.

Witney must have been one of many small settlements formed during the obscurity of the Dark Ages, the first primitive village being sited on a defensible hillock of cornbrash, surrounded by the marshy flood plain of the River Windrush and delineated by the 280ft contour. It seems likely that the widest part of present-day Corn Street marks the centre of the original village settlement, which would have been merely a collection of simple huts. For the next three or four centuries, the inhabitants of the district eked out a precarious existence amid the woods and marshes on either side of the River Windrush.

The original village settlement was known as 'Witta's Island', possibly after a tribal leader. Alternatively, the name may have meant 'White Island', in which case there may be a correlation with the river name 'Windrush', which is thought to have been derived from Gwen-risc, a Celtic name signifying the white stream or morass a reference, perhaps, to abundant white flowers which may once have bloomed along its banks.

The Saxons often gave their villages names reflecting topographical features, and it comes as no surprise to discover that woodland names are very common. Bampton, for instance, means 'Wood' or 'Beam Town', while names containing the words 'ley' or 'leigh' signify woodland clearings. Thus, the outlying hamlets of Crawley and Hailey, to the north of Witney, mean 'Crow Clearing' and 'Hay Clearing' respectively, while North Leigh was obviously the 'North Clearing'.

In the fullness of time, primitive settlements such as Witney developed as the headquarters of small estates which later became manors. In some cases, the estates may have coincided with existing Romano-British estates, implying a degree of continuity between the Roman and Saxon periods. Unlike the Britons, who had followed the Christian religion, the Saxons worshipped Norse gods such as Wodin and Thor. Later, they converted to Christianity, and from then on a network of nucleated parishes was superimposed upon the patchwork of manorial estates.

In many cases the parish boundaries coincided with those of the estates, but sometimes there was a confusing element of overlapping. Nevertheless, it would probably be true to say that most of the early Saxon settlements in West Oxfordshire were based upon existing land units which were both manors and parishes, Witney being a former Roman estate that passed into Saxon control before becoming an ecclesiastical parish.

The Rise of Wessex
The development of Saxon Oxfordshire was disrupted by conflict between Wessex and Mercia, with the likelihood that Wychwood Forest formed a natural barrier between these rival English kingdoms. The situation was further complicated by the appearance of a hybrid group known as the 'Hwicce', who became established in the Cotswold area and gave their name to Wychwood Forest.

The area around the Upper Thames Valley was traditionally part of Wessex, and in this context it is interesting to note that Alfred the Great (849-901) was born just across the county boundary in Wantage, while nearby Dorchester was the headquarters of the ecclesiastical see of Wessex from 634 until 707, when the see was transferred to Winchester.

2 *King Alfred was born at nearby Wantage in 849, and this may explain, at least in part, why the rulers of Wessex were keen to re-conquer the Upper Thames Valley after it had fallen under Mercian control.*

The Upper Thames Valley nevertheless remained an area of immense significance to the rulers of Wessex and in 752 it is recorded that 'This year Cuthred, King of the West Saxons, in the twelfth year of his reign, fought at Burford against Ethelbald, King of the Mercians, and put him to flight.'

The Midland kingdom of Mercia was at its peak during the reign of King Offa (757-96), and much of West Oxfordshire was under Mercian control at that time. In 779 Offa attacked the West Saxon stronghold at Benson 'and captured the vill', the likelihood being that as a result of this victory the Mercians obtained control of all Wessex lands north of the Thames, including Witney. In the event, the power of Mercia was destroyed by an invasion of Danish Vikings, who came from across the North Sea to plunder and burn their way across much of England.

Soon only Wessex remained under English rule, but under Alfred's leadership the West Saxons were able to launch a counter-attack which drove the Danes out of Wessex and southern Mercia. At length, the boundary between English and Danish territory was fixed along the line of Watling Street, and 'English Mercia' was incorporated into an enlarged Wessex encompassing all of Oxfordshire and much of the area further to the north.

Meanwhile, for administrative purposes, England had been sub-divided into a system of shires. This system originated in Wessex and was gradually extended into Mercia and other parts of the country as the West Saxons consolidated their control over the rest of England. By the 10th century, Oxford had been laid out as one of the fortified 'burghs' which King Alfred and his descendants employed in his campaign against the Danes, while the surrounding territory became the newly created county of Oxfordshire.

The Witney Charters

The name Witney was mentioned for the first time in a charter of 969, whereby King Edgar granted the estate to his thegn, Ælfhelm. Three-quarters of a century later, in 1044, a second charter from Edward the Confessor granted the property to Bishop Aelfwine of Winchester. According to a picturesque legend, the grant of 1044 was made in unusual circumstances, insofar as the king's mother, Emma of Normandy (*c*.985-1052), the widow of Ethelred the Unready and the second wife of King Cnut, had been accused of having an improper affair with Bishop Ælfwine. In order to prove that this charge of adultery was groundless, Queen Emma agreed to walk barefoot over nine red-hot ploughshares

3   *Witney Town Hall and Buttercross, looking north towards the High Street, c.1977.*

4   *Witney High Street, c.1951, looking south towards The Hill with St Mary's Parish Church visible in the distance.*

– her willingness to submit herself this terrifying trial by ordeal being taken as a sure sign of total innocence.

Notwithstanding the story of Emma and the fiery ploughshares, the Witney charters are of particular interest in that, in the absence of proper mapping techniques, the boundaries of the estate were delineated with reference to a series of landmarks such as 'Hawks Tumulus' and 'The Old Ford'. The charters of 969 and 1044 therefore provide a glimpse of the local landscape around the end of the first millennium. The charters suggest that the northern parts of the manor was still heavily wooded. For example, the north-western boundary of the Witney estate (where it met the borders of Minster) was known as 'Wood Chipping Way', while the western border between the two estates was defined by prominent landmarks such as 'The Slope where the Nut Trees Grow', 'The High Clearing', and 'Long Clearing Way' (i.e., Langley Way). The southern part of the manorial estate, in contrast, was a damp, marshy area containing places with insalubrious names such as 'Foul Island' and 'Occa's Slippery Place'.

2

Witney in the Medieval Period

L ate Saxon England was one of the richest countries in Europe, and it was perhaps for this reason that, in 1066, it fell victim to William the Conqueror. However, as William I had at least some claim to the throne and he was clever enough to adapt the laws and institutions of England to his own needs, the Norman Conquest did not mark any great break with the past and the existing system of manors, parishes and shires was retained as the basis of Anglo-Norman rule. The main change was that the manors passed into the grasping hands of King William's avaricious followers.

Witney remained an episcopal manor, albeit under a Norman bishop, while the manor of Cogges was given to Wadard, who is depicted as a mounted knight on the famous Bayeux Tapestry. In the event Wadard held the manor for a relatively short period, and within about ten years Cogges had been granted to another Norman family, known as the Arsics.

Witney and Domesday Book

The Domesday Survey of 1086 reveals that Oxfordshire was among the most prosperous counties in England. The largest settlement in the area was the royal manor of Bampton, which had a population of about five hundred. Witney, with Adderbury one of two local manors belonging to the Bishop of Winchester, was somewhat smaller, being a village of 56 householders, meticulously described according to their status as 'serfs', 'villeins' or 'bordars'. Domesday Book described the estate as follows:

> The Bishop of Winchester holds Witney. Archbishop Stigund held it. There are 30 hides. There is land for 24 ploughs. Now in demesne there are 5 ploughs and 9 serfs; and 36 villeins with 11 bordars have 20 ploughs. There are two mills rendering 32s. 6d., and 100 acres of meadowland. There is woodland 3 leagues in length and 2 in breadth. When it is stocked it is worth 50 shillings. In King Edward's time the manor was worth £22. Now it is worth £25.

5 *Wadard, depicted as a mounted knight on the Bayeux Tapestry, under the legend 'Hic est Wadard'.*

The number of 'hides' quoted in relation to an Anglo-Saxon manor will give some idea of its size and relative importance. A hide was a unit of land sufficient to support one freeman and his family. It should be noted that Domesday Book made no mention of the dependent hamlets of Curbridge, Crawley and Hailey, the implication being that these outlying settlements were regarded as integral parts of the manor of Witney.

The population of a Domesday manor can usually be ascertained by reference to the number of households listed in the survey. Assuming that each villein, bordar and serf was a householder, and that an average cottage housed a husband, his wife, two or three children and perhaps an aged parent, it is reasonable to suggest that an average family unit would have comprised at least five people. Thus, by multiplying the number of households by five, we can obtain an approximate population figure for a given settlement. Witney, therefore had an approximate population of around 280 in 56 households.

The contiguous settlement of Cogges was recorded in the Domesday Survey as a separate land holding in the possession of Wadard. Only three serfs were mentioned, which implies a small village of some 15 people living in just three households. There was also a mill rendering 10 shillings, together with meadowland '11 furlongs in length and 2 furlongs in breadth, pasture 3 furlongs in length and 1 furlong in length, and woodland 18 furlongs in length and 6 in breadth'. The size of the manor of Cogges was just five hides.

Witney 'Castle'

Although it was sited at the centre of an important manor, early Norman Witney was merely a small village on a marshy 'island' within the vast expanse of Wychwood Forest. It is assumed that the original Saxon church and manor house were constructed mainly of timber. However, about fifty years after the Norman Conquest, the Bishop of Winchester erected a stone-built manor house at Witney in convenient proximity to the parish church. At the same time, it is possible that urban development was already under way. However, before further progress could be made, the country was disrupted by the outbreak of a vicious civil war.

Henry I, the Conqueror's youngest son, died in 1135 having nominated his daughter Matilda, the window of the German emperor, as his successor. But the Barons decided that a mere woman was unfit to rule and offered the crown to Stephen de Blois, the late King's favourite nephew. This was hardly a wise choice as Stephen lacked the qualities of leadership needed for successful kingship. A chronicler described him as 'a mild man, soft and good', who 'began many things but never finished them'. Taking advantage of England's weakness, the Welsh and Scots raided across the borders, while in September 1139 Matilda invaded the country from Anjou.

For the next 14 years, England was racked by civil war and, freed from any kind of central control, the Anglo-Norman landowners erected private castles and fortifications. At Witney, for instance, Bishop Henry de Blois (c.1096-1171), the king's brother and one of the richest and most powerful men in England, decided to transform his already substantial manor house into a walled and moated castle with a gatehouse and characteristic Norman 'tower-keep' – although in this instance the fortifications were 'adulterine' or unlicensed. Bishop Henry, one of the foremost castle-builders in England, was responsible for building or rebuilding several castles or fortified manor houses, including those at Witney, Wolvesey, Farnham, Downton and Taunton.

By 1141 Stephen's forces were on the verge of defeat, and Matilda was being praised as England's heroine. Unfortunately, her greed and vindictive temper alienated many of those who had supported her and by 1142 the civil war had resumed with a vengeance. At one stage Matilda was besieged in Oxford Castle, and was obliged to escape under cover of darkness before the castle was taken by Stephen's army, while the castles at Radcot and Bampton were attacked and a battle was fought around Radcot Bridge.

Meanwhile, Bishop Henry had apparently completed his building operations at Witney. Excavations carried out in the 1980s suggested that, as first built, the bishop's manor house at Witney had consisted of a rectangular keep and a projecting north range, with an encircling wall or 'enceinte'. These predominantly domestic building were subsequently reinforced by the addition of massive earthworks and a much stronger curtain wall, together with a gatehouse on the northern side of the courtyard. It seems reasonable to assume that these extensive building works were carried out in connection with the military activities taking place around Witney during the 1140s.

6 *The only known illustration of Witney's medieval manor house, from a pen and ink drawing of c.1729 attributed to Nathaniel Buck. The Norman tower-keep can be seen on the right, while the gatehouse is visible to the left. The domestic building in the centre of the picture appears to be largely intact, while the substantial outer walls, although reduced in height, may be the remains of Bishop Henry's fortifications.*

The remodelled manor house sported a moat which may have contained water for all or part of the year, this greatly strengthened house being for all intents and purposes a castle, which could if necessary have been pressed into use for military purposes. The extensive earthworks provided in connection with the rebuilding operations 'entombed' the ground floor of the keep within a mound (or 'mount'), thereby turning the original first floor into the ground floor. It is interesting to note that similar building operations were put into effect at other Winchester castles and manor houses during the troubled reign of Stephen and Matilda, possibly as part of a concerted plan.

The civil war was finally ended by a compromise in 1153, when it was agreed that Stephen would continue to reign until his death, upon which Matilda's son, Henry Plantagenet, would become king. Henry II was duly crowned in 1154, but in the following year Henry de Blois antagonised the new king by going to France without royal authority. The king seized the opportunity to demolish the bishop's unlicensed defence works, Farnham being demilitarised in 1155 while Witney Castle was probably 'slighted' at around the same time – the 1984 excavations revealed that Henry's unauthorised crenellations may have been symbolically tumbled into the moat.

The demilitarised 'castle' retained its tower-keep, together with a hall block and a separate gatehouse on the north side of the enceinte. However, the surrounding walls were breached and possibly reduced in height, making the building untenable as a place of defence for an over-mighty subject such as Bishop Henry. Thereafter, the bishop's manor house at Witney reverted to its earlier role as the headquarters of a manorial estate though, as late as the Victorian period, scholars such as W.J. Monk referred to the half-ruinous building as 'Witney Castle'.

The Bishop's New Town

As lords of the manor of Witney from 1044 until 1862, successive Bishops of Winchester were able to influence the development of the settlement in a variety of ways. At some time in the early 13th century, probably *c*.1208, Bishop Peter de Roches (*c*.1175-1238) decided that Witney would be deliberately expanded as an urban settlement, and to facilitate this ambitious scheme a spacious 'new town' was laid out on a fresh site to the east of the earlier village, a thoroughfare later known as 'Crundell Street' (Corn Street) being created between the old and new parts of the town.

The whole settlement was surrounded by a drainage ditch known as 'Emma's Dyke', and in places the newly created burgage plots were artificially raised above water level. It is thought that the Dyke, which was merely a ditch with no defensive function, originally left the Windrush in an west-north-westerly direction and then flowed beneath the High Street before turning through 180 degrees and rejoining the Windrush to the south of the town.

The new town was aligned from north to south, with long burgage plots extending to the east and west of a wide marketing area, which later became the High Street, Market Square and Church Green. Further burgage plots were created on each side of Corn

Street, which diverged westwards from the High Street, while a lane or trackway ran due east towards the village of Cogges, with a market cross erected at the junction of these nascent streets. At its north end, the High Street merged into the present Bridge Street and West End.

It is noticeable that the 13th-century street plan bears little relation to the island core of Witney, and the axial centre of the bishop's new town (i.e., the area around the market cross) was not coincident with the centre of 'Witta's Island', which was presumably still occupied by the original village settlement. It appears, therefore, that the bishop's new town was purposely laid out on a new site to the east of the original village to avoid unnecessary demolition of existing dwellings.

The new township was planned on what was, by medieval standards, a comparatively generous scale, the distance from St Mary's Church in the south to 'Woodgreen' in the north being around one mile. The River Windrush marked the limits of the town on the east side of the High Street, while on the opposite side the westernmost limit of the main burgage plots was delineated by a 'back lane' running northwards from the widest part of Corn Street to what may originally have been a river crossing at Woodford Mill. It is conceivable that this back lane (later known as 'Puck Lane') was an ancient north-to-south trackway that had run through the original Saxon village and linked it to Hailey in the north and Ducklington in the south.

In the fullness of time, additional building plots were laid out in Corn Street, Bridge Street and West End, although these were much smaller than the original burgage plots;

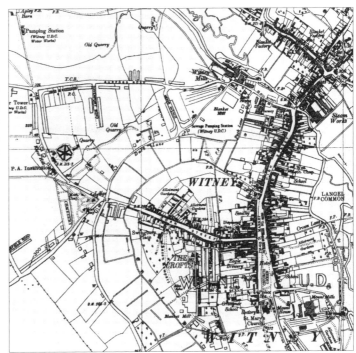

7   The six-inch Ordnance Survey map shows the wedge-shaped marketing area laid out by the Bishop of Winchester running from north-to-south, and Corn Street extending towards the west.

8　*Cogges Church, by local Victorian artist William Seely.*

those on either side of Bridge Street were about one acre in extent, whereas the plots in West End covered about half-an-acre. In the meantime, the evident success of Witney as an urban unit encouraged Robert Arsic, the owner of the adjacent manor of Cogges, to create a similar 'new town' on his land to the north-east and, in this way, the lengthy street known as 'Newland' was brought into existence as an adjunct to the bishop's new town. At the same time, population growth was also taking place in the outlying hamlets of Hailey and Crawley, to the north of Witney, and in Curbridge to the south-west.

As a result of these 13th-century developments, Witney was transformed into a typical English market town, with a clearly defined street plan that has survived intact until the present day. Fairs were founded in 1202 and 1231, taking place on Ascension Day and St Leonard's Day. The number of fairs was subsequently increased to four, with an additional fair in June, and another – known as 'Witney Feast – on the Monday following 8 September.

The new town soon began to prosper and the Hundred Rolls reveal that there were, by the 1270s, around 350 holders of messuages in Witney and in the satellite hamlets of Hailey, Crawley and Curbridge. On the assumption that each family unit comprised two adults and around three children, this would imply a total population of approximately 1,750, of whom about 1,100 lived within the 'borough' of Witney.

Names such as Richard Carpenter, Gilbert Hayward, Edith Dairymaid, Thomas Cobbler, William Smith, Thomas Mercer, Henry Vintner, Richard Dyer and Edmund the Fuller hint at the many trades and occupations carried out within the new town, while surnames also suggest the geographical origins of tenants such as Richard de Ducklington, Ralph de Erdington, Adam Dunstable, Gilbert de Norfolk and John de Combe. Other recorded surnames hint at personal traits, such as Thomas Petit, Adam Crochere

9　*A Victorian print, dedicated to the Rev. Charles Jerram, showing St Mary's Parish Church c.1850. Printed by C. Moody of High Holborn.*

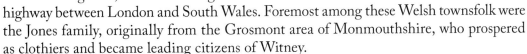

10 *A medieval building said to have been situated in 'Duck Alley' (near the present 53 Corn Street) sketched by William Seely during the Victorian period.*

and Henry Honilove, while others sound decidedly strange to modern ears – Ralph Bukepot, Henry Herringpot, Henry Herring, Richard Sprud and Agnes Prodome being among the oddest names listed in the Hundred Rolls.

There are indications that, by the end of the medieval period, Witney had attracted a number of Welsh immigrants, the town being situated on a main highway between London and South Wales. Foremost among these Welsh townsfolk were the Jones family, originally from the Grosmont area of Monmouthshire, who prospered as clothiers and became leading citizens of Witney.

The ordinary dwelling houses in local towns and villages were single-storey timber-framed buildings with thatched roofs. Chimneys and fireplaces were not provided in these simple dwellings, the smoke from open hearths being allowed to escape through holes in the roof. The largest and most impressive buildings in Witney during the medieval period were the parish church and the adjacent manor house, which are likely to have been the only stone buildings in the town, though as times became more prosperous cloth merchants or other leading townsfolk began to build additional stone buildings, some of which would have been two stories high, amid the ordinary single-storey houses.

11 *A Seely sketch purporting to show the 12th-century rectory prior to its demolition.*

12 *A c.1912 postcard view of Newland, looking east towards Oxford Hill. This picturesque old street was part of Cogges.*

Local Government

As far as can be ascertained, medieval Witney was an unincorporated borough, and despite a reference to the townsfolk making a payment of 40s. for a 'charter' from Peter de Roches in 1210, no charter has survived to record precisely what was granted. Nevertheless, the burgesses of Witney were allowed a considerable degree of autonomy, the township being governed largely through a borough court with elected bailiffs, although the bishop continued to exercise control though his own bailiff and a twice-yearly manorial court. Witney was thus a seigniorial borough which enjoyed significant liberties, the rights afforded to its inhabitants being analogous to those allowed in other new towns such as Farnham and Taunton.

In 1256 a later bishop granted a charter to Newtown on the Isle of Wight and gave it all the liberties and freedoms of his burgesses at Taunton, Witney, Alresford and Farnham. These privileges, as set out in a Farnham charter of 1249, included the right to hold their own court before their own bailiffs; the right to make all attachments and distraints; freedom from attending any other of the bishop's courts except his twice-yearly hundred courts; the receipt of tolls from fairs and fines from the assizes of bread and ale; and the right to issue summonses.

Origins of the Witney Blanket Industry

It could be argued that the Middle Ages were a time of slow but steady progress. Indeed, modern England was largely created between the years 1200 and 1500. In those three centuries, land was laboriously won for agricultural cultivation, the cloth industry was slowly developed, towns were founded and learning steadily progressed. By the end of the 15th century, Witney had an estimated population of about 1,500 and had grown into a prosperous market town.

The one major setback during this time was the Black Death of 1349, which checked population growth and caused the depopulation of villages such as Yelford and Caswell (near Curbridge). As far as Witney is concerned, 13 vacant houses were recorded in 1348-9, suggesting that the great pestilence had resulted in a shortage of tenants. On the other hand, it is generally agreed that the Black Death assisted the growth of a money-based economy by lessening the power of feudal landlords and increasing the bargaining power of the labouring classes. It also encouraged the growth of large-scale sheep farming, especially in the Cotswolds, and this in turn prepared the way for the creation of an important textile industry in the years to come. At the same time, as people moved from farming villages to urban settlements such as Witney and Chipping Norton, these towns began to flourish as regional marketing and trading centres.

Despite claims of greater antiquity, it seems that the famous Witney blanket industry originated, on a small scale, during the Middle Ages, when the wool from local sheep flocks supplied large numbers of domestic spinners and weavers. It is likely that Witney became a specialised cloth-making centre as weavers sought to escape from the restrictive guild regulations in old-established 'industrial' towns such as Coventry. The Pipe Rolls refer to a fine of 6s. 8d. inflicted upon a Witney weaver in 1179, while *The Cartulary of Eynsham Abbey* records the sale of fleeces to a Witney wool merchant in 1268.

Traditionally, the raw wool was spun into yarn on domestic spinning wheels, and in medieval times many local people earned their livings from a mixture of spinning and farming. Weaving was carried out in Witney on handlooms, located in ordinary houses and cottages, while spinning was undertaken over a wide area of the Cotswolds, these processes being organised on a purely domestic basis. Only the finishing process known as 'fulling' was mechanised, and this took place in water-powered fulling or 'tucking' mills, which were sited at regular intervals along the fast-flowing River Windrush. Manorial records indicate that there were at least three fulling mills in Witney during the 13th century, one of these being 'New Mill', while the others were known as 'Woodford Mill' and 'Waleys Mill'.

The Parish Church

The parish church of St Mary is an impressive cruciform structure incorporating a nave, chancel, central tower, aisles, transepts and two-storeyed porch. The building measures approximately 130ft from north to south and 130ft across the transepts from east to west, while the tower has a height of 156ft. The heads of two blocked round-headed windows in the nave suggest that the first stone church, which was probably erected during the 11th century, comprised a nave and chancel, while the north aisle, with its characteristic Norman doorway, was presumably a 12th-century addition. The church was greatly enlarged during the 13th century, when it acquired north and south transepts, a south nave aisle and a new chancel, the transepts having western aisles.

It is assumed that the central tower, with its magnificent spire, was also added during the 13th century, though it may be worth mentioning that the ringing chamber within the tower contains an unusual mural passage or triforium, which runs around three sides of the tower and is pierced by triangular-headed openings not unlike the windows in Saxon churches such as that at Earls Barton. The tower also contains some 'herring bone' stonework, which may also indicate greater antiquity.

13 *(Above) St Mary's parish church as depicted in a drawing by the Witney architect William Wilkinson. Holloway's Almshouses, to the left of the church, were rebuilt to a design by Wilkinson in 1868.*

14 *A detailed view of St Mary's Church, showing the Decorated window at the south end of the south transept. The blocked arch formerly gave access to a chantry chapel, which was converted into a sexton's house after the Reformation and was demolished in 1821.*

15 *A recent view of St Mary's Church, one of the finest ecclesiastical buildings in the county. Its rather bleak interior is a result of Tudor iconoclasm and Victorian restoration, although this gaunt austerity, which is perhaps appropriate for Puritan Witney, serves to emphasise the grandeur of the mainly Early English architecture. Externally, the building is magnificent, and the soaring 156ft spire can be seen for miles around.*

The Outlying Hamlets and Witney Park

As mentioned above, the manor of Witney contained the hamlets of Hailey, Crawley and Curbridge, as well as the borough – the geography of the area being such that these outlying settlements impinged on the 'urban' parts of the town. In fact, the relationship between Witney, Cogges and the outlying hamlets was decidedly complicated, insofar as Newland belonged to Cogges and Woodgreen was part of Hailey. The Bishop's Deer Park was, similarly, part of Curbridge, and all of these areas were outside the jurisdiction of the borough court.

References to Witney 'Park' first occur during the mid-13th century, when the Bishop of Winchester laid out a deer park in what was still a well-wooded area to the west of what is now Tower Hill. The park extended as far west as the present Downs Road, while its northern boundary was delineated by the Burford Road. The park was surrounded by a dry ditch and a substantial stone wall which, in later years, became partially obscured by hedgerows. Although the ditch and wall have now largely disappeared, the hedgerow has survived in several places – notably along the cycle path beside the Burford Road and beside the footpath from Tower Hill to the Windrush Valley Housing Estate. The park was equipped with a 'hall' or 'grange', which may have been used as a hunting lodge by the Bishop of Winchester and his aristocratic friends.

16 *The Wenman Chapel, at the north-western end of St Mary's Church, recalls a famous Witney wool-trading family of the medieval era. This monument to William Wenman was one of several family monuments which were apparently destroyed when the Wenman Chapel was adapted for use an infants' school around 1840.*

3

The Tudor and Early Stuart Periods

There was no decisive break between the medieval and Tudor periods, and the Middle Ages did not simply end after the Wars of the Roses. There was nevertheless a rupture with the past after the Black Death in 1349, which checked population growth and weakened both the feudal nobility and the Roman Catholic Church, but both of these institutions survived intact until the Tudor period.

Increasing Prosperity

Meanwhile, a growing 'middling class' of merchants and yeomen were quietly yet inexorably building up the nation's wealth. The late 15th and early 16th centuries were a time of rising prosperity and the burgeoning merchant classes were able to exploit the growing market for high-quality wool and woollen products. In these years, 'new men' such as Walter Jones (d. 1560), Richard Wenman (d. 1534) and Thomas Box (c.1552-96) were gradually assimilated into the gentry class, while older families such as the Lovells of Minster Lovell became extinct. In 1602 Walter Jones, who had received a generous inheritance from his uncle Walter, was able to purchase Chastleton House in North Oxfordshire, while the Wenmans were wealthy enough to endow their own chapel in the north aisle of Witney parish church.

Witney was still governed by the borough court although, from the late 15th century onwards, the Bishops of Winchester had leased their demesne lands at Witney to the Brice family, who occupied the old manor house and remained as tenants until the Cromwellian period. The manor court retained its jurisdiction over the satellite hamlets, and for outlying parts of Witney such as Woodgreen.

Wills and probate inventories are invaluable sources of information in relation to Tudor and Stuart Witney. Probate inventories, made for the purpose of proving wills and safeguarding the administrators from charges of fraud, contain useful details of houses, furniture, tools, clothes and other possessions, and as such they provide a glimpse of everyday life in the 15th and 16th centuries.

17 *A drawing by William Seely showing a Tudor building on the east side of Market Square. The structure was demolished in the 1860s to make way for the Corn Exchange. It is conceivable that this property may have formed part of an earlier* White Hart Inn, *although the 1839-40 tithe map places the* White Hart *in Bridge Street.*

As far as buildings are concerned, the inventories reveal that the houses of the period would typically have contained a 'hall', or living room, and one or more 'chambers' or bedrooms, often sited above the hall. There were in addition 'parlours', 'bakehouses', 'butteries' and a variety of subsidiary buildings, many of which were used for weaving, tanning or other 'industrial' activities.

The lengthy inventory of Thomas Taylor the Elder, dated 24 October 1583, suggests that, although of 'yeoman' status, Thomas had been a comparatively wealthy man who lived in a large and complex house. The inventory lists the following locations, all of which appear to have been on the ground floor of the main house:

> Hall with wooden panelling and three glazed windows
> Buttery within the Hall
> Store House
> The New Parlour with wood panelling and two glazed windows
> The Old Parlour with wood panelling and two glazed windows
> The Buttery within the Old Parlour

18 *A Seely drawing of an 'Elizabethan house' in the High Street, later known as Pinnacle House. This house became the home of Dame Marriott, the widow of a well-known 18th-century blanket-maker.*

19 *Another Seely drawing showing a large Tudor property on the east side of Church Green, which is said to have been used as a 'Plague Retreat' by the Fellows of Corpus Christi College. Most of these large Tudor buildings were parallel to the street.*

The hall and parlours contained various furniture, including two long tables, benches, a 'round table with six stools', cupboards, built-in settles, pewter, trenchers and fire irons. Having listed the contents of the ground-floor domestic rooms, the compilers of the inventory seem to have moved upstairs to the bed chambers, which were well-furnished with bedsteads, bedding, cushions, curtains and chests. The specified locations on the upper floor were as follows:

> The Chamber over the Buttery
> The Geasten (Guests') Chamber
> The Chamber over the New Parlour
> The Chamber over the Hall
> The Chamber over the New Buttery
> The Gallery
> The Closet near the Gallery

Having descended a staircase 'with glazed window', the testators then described the extensive yards, outhouses and close, which evidently extended as far as the River Windrush. Interestingly, Thomas Taylor's possessions included 'an arming coate, a livery bowe with twoo sheaffe of arrowes, a calliver, a flaske and a touche boxe and a heade peece', together with two rusty swords and a 'forrest byll'. The presence of this military equipment suggest that the deceased man had served in the local 'Trained Band' or militia unit.

Nicholas Hill's inventory, made on 15 January 1589/90, refers to a hall with 'Buttrye within', a parlour, a 'Naperye', the 'Yeling House next to the Hall' (a brewhouse), the 'Chamber over the entry' and chambers over the hall, parlour and 'Yeling house', together with a bakehouse, stable, courtyard and close. The precise location of Nicholas Hill's house is unknown although, as there are references to hop poles and 'the olde tymber that is lefte of the olde Brydge' that was stored as 'the Rivers syde', it seems likely that this extensive property must have occupied one of the large burgage plots on the east side of Church Green or the High Street.

Thomas Taylor and Nicholas Hill were clearly among the most successful men in the town. At the other end of the social scale, smaller tradesmen such as Gregory Merryman, who died in 1596, were still living in simple cottage-type properties comprising a 'hall', chamber and a 'little chamber', together with a buttery and kitchen.

Everyday Life in Tudor Witney

The Court Books of the borough of Witney are another useful source of information about the everyday life of the town during the Tudor period. Two surviving books, covering the period 1538-1609, contain records of the administrative business performed by the bailiffs, together with records of various judicial proceedings conducted in the borough courts in relation to debts and similar matters. In addition, the borough court dealt with apprenticeship indentures, offences against the Assize of Bread and Ale, and other minor transgressions.

In general, the borough court conducted the kind of business that was later carried out by the county councils and quarter sessions – in July 1552, for example, it was ordered that all dogs and bitches should be muzzled, while in 1566 'no pigs over a quarter of a year old' were to be allowed in the streets unless ringed 'on pain of 3s. 4d. for each pig'. An order of June 1582 required every householder in Witney to 'have standing or set without his street door on every night … one tub, cowl, barrel, pail, pan or cauldron with water in readiness for necessity against fire on pain of 6d. for every default to the contrary'.

The officers of the borough court comprised two bailiffs, a 'Sergeant-of-the-Mace', two constables and five 'wardsmen', the equivalent of modern councillors. There were in addition a number of minor officers such as leather-sealers, cloth searchers and ale-tasters. The wardsmen represented the town's five wards which, in the Tudor period, were 'Paternoster Row' on the west side of Church Green; 'East Ward' on the east side of the Green; 'West Ward' to the west of the High Street; 'Middle Ward' comprising the remaining part of the High Street; and 'Beneath the Bridge Ward', which encompassed those parts of the borough to the north of the river.

20 *A Seely illustration of Witney's four-arched medieval bridge. The bridge was later reconstructed with three arches.*

21 *Witney High Street, looking north, with 'Pinnacle House' visible to the left. Although dating from 1828, this 19th-century view shows a number of 16th- or 17th-century buildings, all of which were built on medieval burgage plots.*

It is interesting to find that the main streets of the town were already known by their modern names. There were, for example, frequent references to the High Street, Bridge Street, Woodgreen Hill, Woodgreen, Newland and Mill Lane. West End was occasionally referred to as 'West End Street', while Corn Street was known variously as 'Crundell Street', 'Crondell Street' or 'Crondall Street'. It appears, however, that 'Corn Street' was becoming the most usual appellation; in December 1575, for instance, there is mention of 'Crondell Street, most commonly called Corne Street' while in December 1603 the Court Books refer to 'Crundall Street, alias Corn Street'. References to the 'West Crofts' or the 'ground called the Crofts' show that this name was already in use to describe the area of land to the south of Corn Street.

The borough's Court Books record the names and occupations of numerous Witney people, roughly half of whom appear to have been connected with the blanket industry. Many of these individuals, including Thomas Puckforde, William Hobson, Henry Brygfeelde, Richard Cakebread, William Bryan, Harry Dey, Gregory Merryman and Henry Gould were described as broadweavers, whereas Richard Okeley and Nicholas Shorter were dyers, William Hunte was a cardmaker and Moses Muckwell a fuller.

The most successful and prosperous weavers, such as Richard Jonson, were described as 'clothiers', although other individuals, such as Thomas Webley and John Clarke, were referred to as both clothiers and broadweavers. This implies that, like many leading members of the Witney blanket industry during the pre-industrial period, these men were 'small masters' who had served their apprenticeships and then gone into business as independent traders employing their own apprentices.

The Buttercross and other Notable Buildings

The junction between Corn Street and Market Square formed a natural meeting place at which people could meet to sell or barter goods. Markets were originally held in the open

air, but when a market cross was erected at this central meeting place the local traders were able to lay out their goods on the stepped platform at the base of the cross. Many market crosses were later provided with simple wooden covers, though in other places, such as Salisbury and Dunster, more elaborate structures were erected.

It is unclear when Witney's market cross became the present Buttercross. This still extant structure appears to be of post-Reformation origin, the likeliest explanation being that the familiar gabled roof covering was erected after the removal of the original cross, which would have been regarded as an idolatrous symbol of Popery in Puritan Witney. In 1606, Richard Ashcombe, a gentleman of Curbridge, left £50 to the bailiffs of Witney to be 'bestowed and layed-out in the building of an house over and above the Crosse of Witney'. However, the 13 stout pillars which support the roof structure appear to be far older than the 16th or 17th century, and it is conceivable that the Buttercross may have had a medieval predecessor. An inscription high on the cupola refers to the installation of the clock by William Blake of Cogges in 1683.

Mention of a 'school master' named Andrew Plandon among the occupants of Tudor Witney in 1552 suggests that a school may have existed in Witney long before the foundation of the grammar school in the following century. The location of the school is unknown, although it is conceivable that teaching may have been conducted in private houses or in premises adapted for use as a 'schoolhouse'.

The growing wealth of Tudor and Stuart England resulted in a great increase in internal trade and travel and this, in turn, encouraged the development of inns and taverns as places in which farmers, carriers and merchants could meet to do business. Market towns such as Witney

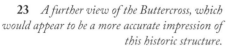

23   *A further view of the Buttercross, which would appear to be a more accurate impression of this historic structure.*

acquired needed large numbers of these establishments – the *White Hart* being Witney's most important inn during the Tudor period.

John Leland, the Tudor antiquary, who passed through Witney and Crawley around 1532, described 'Whitney' as a market town, its 'fayre churche' having a 'goodly piramis of stone', while at 'Crauley' he found a 'Bridge of two arches of stone over Winruche river, that goithe by Whitney'. Witney Bridge, linking the High Street and Bridge Street, was of similar design, albeit with four arches.

The Reformation and the Puritan Tradition

In medieval times Witney had been a Roman Catholic town; there was simply no other choice. Moreover, men and women were unable to visualise a 'multi-faith' society, and in these circumstances it was considered that all people should belong to one supra-national church. Dissenters, who were regarded as 'heretics', risked being burned at the stake.

The origins of English Protestantism can be traced back to the 14th-century Lollards, who questioned Catholic orthodoxy and anticipated many of the key doctrines of the Reformation. Driven underground, Lollardy survived in many clothing towns. In the early 1520s a Lollard activist known as 'Old Father Hacker' was distributing 'heretical' tracts in Burford, and it seems likely that these tracts would have found their way to Witney, where a group of local people, including a man called 'Gune' who was given 'a Book of the Ten Commandments', were receptive to the new ideas. The Catholics responded by punishing townsfolk such as John Gunn and John Baker, who were accused of reading heretical material, while John Brabant was denounced by his own son 'for reading a certain English book of scripture, and so condemned them all, including his own parents, to be branded on the cheek and to stand upon the highest step of the Cross of Burford with faggotts upon their shoulders for a quarter of an hour on market day'.

Undeterred by Catholic persecution, the rising yeoman and merchant classes of early Tudor England tended to support Protestant forms of worship, and for this reason there were few objections in West Oxfordshire when Henry VIII made his historic break with Rome during the 1530s and turned England into a Protestant state. It is interesting to discover that Thomas Wolsey, who as Bishop of Winchester had been associated with Witney, was later accused of seizing property in the manor and borough of Witney for his own use, an accusation made during his trial in 1530.

The people of the area became enthusiastic supporters of the reformed faith, and a major step towards the creation of a Protestant national church was a letter sent to the bishops in 1538, urging them exhort the laity to read the Bible and to set a date by which each parish church would have an English Bible for public reading. An authoritative translation, known as *The Great Bible*, was printed in 1539, and by 1541 it had run through no less than five editions.

There were, nevertheless, some vociferous opponents of the reforms, among them a Mr Don of Corpus Christi College, Oxford, who objected to the Bible being read during meal times at his college. Foolishly, in 1538 Mr Don made his anti-Reformation views known while preaching in Witney church. He opined that, 'in the old time, good men were wont to build churches, but now they were more ready to pluck them down'. He also asserted that 'men make laws now for money, not for the commonweal'. Inevitably, these anti-Protestant views were reported to the university authorities, with the result that the hapless Mr Don was severely censured.

The Tudor reformers envisaged a the creation of broad national Church of England that would embrace all worshippers, but religious dissent continued unabated, with the nature of that church, and its forms of worship, being much debated. The most enthusiastic Protestants, who wished to 'purify' the Church and cast away the last trappings of Popery and superstition, were known as the Puritans – although Puritanism itself took many forms. Attempts to impose Catholicism by force during the reign of Mary I served only to strengthen support for the Protestant cause, and in the ensuing years clothing towns such as Witney became strongholds of Puritanism.

Although in broad terms the Tudor period was a time of progress and consolidation for West Oxfordshire, external events such as the war with Spain impinged on everyday life from time to time. At moments of particular crisis men were called up to serve in the defence forces under the traditional system, whereby each district was obliged to provide its quota of trained personnel. In 1542, for instance, the parish of Witney was required to furnish 70 archers and bill-men, while in 1580 Oxfordshire was able to provide 5,000 armed men to repel an expected Spanish invasion. Intriguingly, the State Papers record that 'Thomas Wenman of Wytney Park' had refused to 'furnish one light horse for Her Majesty's service, he being of ability and living meet for the same', suggesting that he may have been a Catholic sympathiser, who supported Spain and its detested Inquisition.

Bartholemew Steare and The 'Witney Rising'

In the 1590s a recession in the clothing industry coincided with a series of poor harvests. At the same time there was growing resentment about the piecemeal enclosure of common land, and against this background of mounting discontent an abortive uprising took place in Oxfordshire in 1596, one of the ring-leaders being Bartholemew Steare of Hampton Poyle, who claimed that 'a hundred good men' would come out of Witney 'to knock down the gentlemen and rich men that take in the commons and make corn so dear'. Alarmingly, he also asserted that 'there was a mason who could make balls of wild-fire, and had a sling to fire the same, whereby he could fire houses as occasion should serve'.

Subsequent enquiries revealed that much of this was pure fantasy. A gentleman of Cogges reported that he had detected no signs whatsoever of an armed insurrection in Witney, while Bartholemew's brother, John Steare of Witney, stated that, although there were undoubtedly good men in Witney, they had taken no part in the failed rising, and he had, moreover, argued with his deluded brother and 'tried to persuade him against such unlawful courses'.

4

The Civil War and the Protectorate

The origins of the Civil War are complex, but briefly, it can be said that social, economic and religious problems engendered political tensions between King Charles I and his Parliament. The war was started by a rebellion in Ireland in November 1641 and, while the King and Parliament argued about raising an army to subdue the rebels, terrified Protestants fled to England, spreading stories of massacres and carnage. These tales lost nothing in the retelling, and England was soon in a state of near-panic. With the Spanish Armada and the persecution of Protestants under Queen Mary still a vivid folk memory, terrified English Protestants expected an Irish invasion.

The unfortunate Irish refugees were seen as the advance guard of a Papist horde, and local sources record an 'Irishwoman' in the parish of Witney during the winter of 1641-2. The lady in question was probably a Protestant of English origin, and one hopes that this victim of ethnic cleansing was well treated (though by analogy with other parishes, this would not necessarily have been the case). Against this background of rising hysteria, the King and his opponents began preparations for war.

The Civil War

Hostilities began on 22 August 1642, and the first large battle took place at Edgehill, near Banbury, on 23 October. The battle was inconclusive, but it enabled the King to establish his wartime capital in Oxford. For the next four years Oxford was in a state of siege, though the Parliamentarians made no attempt to storm the city, and it appears that local people could come and go more or less as they pleased. The Witney clothiers maintained their commercial links with the Parliamentary stronghold of London, although trade was disrupted and the countryside was scoured by Royalist troops who claimed the right to demand food and sequester 'rebel' property.

The sympathies of the Oxfordshire as a whole were probably with the Parliament. Many Parliamentary leaders, including John Hampden (1594-1643), Speaker William

24 *An engraving of the House of Commons showing William Lenthall (1591-1662) in the Speaker's Chair. In 1642 Speaker Lenthall, who became lord of the manor of Witney during the Commonwealth period, bravely defied Charles I by refusing to hand over five Members accused of treason.*

Lenthall (1591-1662) and Lord Saye and Sele (1582-1662) resided within the county or had properties in the area, while woollen towns such as Witney were invariably centres of extreme Protestantism and would naturally have supported the Parliamentary cause.

There were at least two local Parliamentary regiments at the start of the war; these were Lord Saye and Sele's Blue Coats and John Hampden's Green Coats; the latter regiment was later incorporated into the New Model Army as Ingoldsby's Regiment. Apart from these locally raised regiments, each area maintained its 'Trained Band' as a sort of Home Guard which was supposed to turn out in times of emergency. Outside London, however, the Trained Bands had become more of a national joke than a national defence force, and there is no evidence that the townsfolk of Witney took their military duties seriously.

There were, from time to time, moments of sudden activity when soldiers from one side or the other marched through the area, the Royalists wearing prominent red sashes and the opposing Parliamentary forces orange sashes to distinguish each side from their enemy (who otherwise wore identical clothing and equipment).

By 1643 Royalist victories elsewhere in the country had resulted in Oxford becoming a place of incarceration for Parliamentarian prisoners, and it is recorded that after the capture of Cirencester over a thousand prisoners were roped together and marched barefoot to Oxford, being confined in various churches en route. At Witney, the strongly Protestant townsfolk attempted to feed the prisoners through the windows of the church, but the Royalist soldiers drew their weapons and callously prevented this small act of mercy. The King, angry because his rebellious Witney subjects had been 'over kind to the Cirencester prisoners', showed his displeasure by demanding cloth for his soldiers from every clothier in the town.

Meanwhile, the cavaliers had adopted a policy of disarming the Trained Bands in areas with Puritan sympathies, and on 8 December 1643 the King's men descended on Witney and collected a variety of weapons, including 36 muskets, 23 bandoliers, 17 'long pikes', six swords, one barrel of gunpowder and one barrel of 'muskett shott'. They also relieved the townsfolk of six breastplates, five backplates and six 'headpeeces', together with one broken sword. This haul of weapons would have equipped a trained band of about 60 infantrymen, comprising musketeers, pikemen (in the ratio of two to one), sergeants and a captain. In the following February 'plankes, boards and spokes, etc.' were collected from Witney for the King's artillery train.

In June 1644 King Charles, fearing that he might become trapped at Oxford, left the beleaguered city with '3,000 horse, each with a musketeer behind him', this army of 6,000 men being accompanied by 'two pieces of cannon and thirty coaches'. Travelling via Handborough, the King's army passed through Witney on the night of 3-4 June 1644. Later, on 18 June, the King marched from Burford to Witney, where he was joined by other Royalist forces.

Further details of these troop movements are provided by the diarist Richard Symonds, a member of the Royalist forces, who recorded that 'His Majestie had been at church and

25 *A reasonable likeness of Sir William Waller who, in early June 1644, pursued the King through West Oxfordshire. The State Papers relate that General Waller 'came on Tuesday night to Witney, by reason of which nearness the King tarried not at Burford, but went away that night'.*

26 *Charles I, as depicted in a woodcut of c.1648. The King was accommodated in* The White Hart *inn during his three-day sojourn in Witney between 18 and 20 July 1644.*

Dauentry   Brimidgham

The most Illustrious and High borne PRINCE RUPERT, PRINCE ELECTOR, Second Son to FREDERICK KING of BOHEMIA, GENERALL of the HORSE of H's MAJESTIES ARMY, KNIGHT of the Noble Order of the GARTER.

27 *A 17th-century illustration purporting to show Prince Rupert, the King's German nephew, who was active in and around Oxford during the First Civil War.*

28 *A poor depiction of Oliver Cromwell, as shown in a broadsheet commemorating a Parliamentary success during the early part of the Civil War. General Cromwell is also supposed to have dined in the* White Hart.

heard the sermon and dyned' before he 'marched to Witney that night'. After three days, the combined force moved northwards via Woodstock to meet the Parliamentarians at the Battle of Cropredy Bridge, near Banbury. It is said that, during his wartime visits to Witney, the King was accommodated at the *White Hart*, at that time the town's most prestigious inn.

Apart from these sudden (and probably unexpected) appearances of entire armies on the march, Witney had a quiet Civil War until 1645, by which time the New Model Army had tipped the balance in favour of Parliament. Ably led by Sir Thomas Fairfax (1612-71), this new army soon achieved major victories over the Cavaliers, but Oxford and other Royalist strongholds still held out and Oliver Cromwell (1599-1658), the commander of the New Model Cavalry, was ordered to eliminate the Royalist garrisons around Oxford. (It is said that, like King Charles before him, General Cromwell dined at the *White Hart* inn during his brief sojourns at Witney.)

The Royalists were left in possession of Oxford for the time being, but in the following year Fairfax laid siege to Oxford and the Royalist outposts in the area. Woodstock finally capitulated on 26 April, while Banbury was liberated on 8 May. Finally, on 24 June 1646 Oxford surrendered without bloodshed, and the first Civil War came to an end.

The Protectorate

It was hoped that the King and Parliament would settle their differences but, sadly, this did not happen, and in 1648 King Charles led his followers into the Second Civil War. As a result of this renewed conflict the King was put on trial, found guilty of high treason and beheaded in London on 30 January 1649. On 19 May England was declared 'A Commonwealth and Free State' by the authority of 'the representatives of the people in Parliament'. Conflict continued in Ireland and Scotland, and in this context there was a final flurry of activity in 1651, when the Prince of Wales led a Scottish army into England. The invaders were, however, routed at the Battle of Worcester on 3 September 1651. The army was now all-powerful, and on 16 December 1653 Oliver Cromwell was declared 'Lord Protector of the Commonwealth of England, Scotland and Ireland'.

Meanwhile, the changing political situation had important ramifications for Witney which, since the days of the Anglo-Saxons,

29 *The arms of 'the Commonwealth of England, Scotland and Ireland'.*

had belonged to the Bishop of Winchester. The Bishop's estates were sequestered in 1647 and the manor subsequently passed into the hands of William Lenthall, the Speaker of the Long Parliament who had famously defied King Charles in 1642. The manor of Witney thereby came into the possession of a leading Parliamentarian although, in view of the Puritan sentiment which seems to have prevailed amongst the townsfolk, this change of ownership may not have been entirely unwelcome.

Overall, the Cromwellian period was a time of peace and reconstruction in Witney. Trade returned to normal and it seems likely that ordinary people welcomed the stability of the new republican government. Unfortunately, there seems to have been a disproportionate number of bigots and busybodies at large in Puritan communities, and in these circumstances mischief-makers were able to inflict real damage on their enemies by making false accusations to those in authority, Stephen Brice and the Rev. Ralph Brideoake being among the victims.

Stephen Brice, the Witney Cavalier

Although Witney played little part in the military history of the period, it is conceivable that Witney men served in one or other of the contending armies; in April 1643, for example, several local men enlisted in the King's army, while it is likely that this Puritan clothing town would have furnished at least some volunteers for the Parliamentarian forces. Frustratingly, there are no records of any local Roundheads, though Stephen Brice of Witney Park is known to have served as a Royalist officer.

In general, those who had fought for the King were well treated by the victorious Parliamentarians – indeed many Royalist soldiers were given cash payments so they could make their way home. Only the most incorrigible 'delinquents' or 'Papists' were punished by Parliament – the preferred methods of retribution being financial rather than corporeal. The sequestration of Cavaliers' property was initially introduced as a means of raising money for the war effort. At first, sequestration was carried out by local committees, but these were later replaced by 'The Committee for Compounding at Goldsmiths' Hall', which allowed delinquent Cavaliers to pay fines. In this way, the state was able to raise significant sums of money from its former enemies. Indeed, between 1644 and 1652 no less than £1,304,957 was received from former Royalists in the form of 'compositions'.

Stephen Brice was examined by the Committee for Compounding on 24 October 1650. Although he had escaped sequestration, this former Royalist officer was clearly still in deep trouble. It was revealed that he had been in arms for the King in 1643 and was said to have deserted in 1644. Since that time 'he had lived peaceably'. However, there was to be no escape and on 4 November 1650 Stephen Brice was fined at 'one sixth', entailing a bill for £49 13s. 4d.

From this bare fact it may be deduced that Stephen Brice was a comparatively wealthy individual, but the reason why he had been pursued so stubbornly by the Parliamentarians remains less clear. If, as he claimed, Mr Brice had deserted from the King's army, he cannot have harboured particularly Royalist views. Neither does he appear to have been a

Roman Catholic, and for this reason religion cannot have played any part in his supposed offences against the state.

There is a third possibility, which is that Stephen Brice may have been the victim of a personal vendetta. The fact that he had been a Royalist soldier would not in itself have led to a charge of 'delinquency', but if one or more individuals – perhaps business rivals from pre-war days – had made such an accusation, however slight, a case against him might have been made. Although it is an unattractive thought, one is led to the conclusion that personal malice may have played a part in the misfortunes of Stephen Brice, the Witney cavalier.

A 'Cavalier and a dull Preacher'

On 8 January 1655 Colonel Thomas Kelsey appeared before the Lord Protector's Council of State in London with what was quaintly described as 'a complaint of some honest men of Witney' about Ralph Brideoake (1613-78), their minister of religion, who had been appointed rector of Witney through the patronage of William Lenthall. Those present included Major-General John Lambert, Major-General George Skippon and other Puritan notables. It appeared that the 'honest men of Witney' had fallen out with their minister, who was said to have been a 'dull preacher' whose theology was based upon 'unsound doctrines'. In 17th-century parlance this implied that his brand of religion was not sufficiently Puritan in tone but, perhaps more importantly, Ralph Brideoake was also accused of being a Cavalier!

It transpired that Mr Brideoake had been chaplain to the Earl of Derby and as such had been present at the second siege of Latham House between May and December 1645. Old Latham House, near Ormskirk in Lancashire, was a strongly defended castle with nine towers and a wide moat. It had given the Parliamentary forces many problems and its defenders would thus have acquired a certain notoriety in Puritan circles. Mr Brideoake's role in the siege had clearly made him a suspicious character, and Colonel Thomas Fothergill, a 'gentleman of Norfolk', was asked to investigate the affair.

At this stage the story becomes decidedly suspicious. Colonel Fothergill claimed that when part of the Royalist garrison at Latham House, Mr Brideoake had urged the Earl of Derby to kill a Parliamentarian prisoner-of-war, advising the Earl to 'hang him up' because he was 'a Puritan rogue'. However, the colonel had not heard these damning words with his own ears: he had heard the story from his grocer, and the evidence was no more than unsubstantiated gossip. As in the case of Stephen Brice, there were suspicions of a personal vendetta, and as Mr Brideoake had promised that he would do nothing in Witney 'without the consent of the honest people there' the council let the matter drop.

Disaster at the White Hart Inn

An incident that occurred in February 1653, after the bailiffs had tried to prevent a group of amateur actors from performing the Elizabethan play *A Most Pleasant Comedy of Mucedorus*, provides further evidence of the distinctly Puritan atmosphere that prevailed in Witney during the days of the Protectorate. Having been barred from the town hall, the rustic thespians staged their performance in a malting house behind the *White Hart*, but disaster struck when the floor gave way, killing five people outright and injuring many more. Those killed at the scene were all children, but a woman died later following the amputation of one of her legs. Instead of sympathy, the sufferers were condemned by John Rowe (1626-77), Witney's Puritan 'Lecturer', who published an account of the occurrence entitled *Tragi-Comœdia; being a brief relation of the strange and wonderful hand of God discovered at Witney in the Comedy acted there.*

While conceding that the tragedy had been 'one of the saddest and blackest nights that ever came upon Witney', Rowe used the disaster to launch an attack upon the theatre by asserting that the play (at one time attributed to William Shakespeare) contained 'scurrilous, impious, blasphemous' passages, including 'a bitter taunt against all Godly persons under the name of Puritans'; in it a player named Comedy urged that 'music revives and mirth is tolerable' but was attacked by Envy who threatened 'a tragic end'. This prediction, commented Rowe, was 'made good by the Divine Hand', for at the close of Act II 'it pleased God to put a stop to their mirth, and by an immediate hand of His own, in causing the chamber to sink, and fall under them, to put an end to this ungodly play'.

Henry Box and the Foundation of Witney Grammar School

There was a widespread belief in education during the Commonwealth period, and many Puritans hoped that money confiscated from the Cavaliers could be used for educational purposes. These ideas were never fully implemented, although the Cromwellian regime was a time of educational progress; one authority has concluded that 'by 1660 educational opportunities were more widespread and stronger than they had ever been before'.

The foundation of Witney Grammar School in 1660 was a notable event at the very end of the Cromwellian period. It was built and endowed by Henry Box (1585-1662), a member of a prominent Witney family who had been apprenticed to the Grocers' Company and prospered in the City of London, and wished to endow a grammar school in his native town.

The first steps were taken in the 1650s, when Henry Box purchased a suitable piece of land near the parish church from Thomas Collier, the blanket-maker. A 'very fair house' was probably under construction by 1660 (or possibly slightly earlier). The new schoolhouse was a large hip-roofed building which may have been inspired by Coleshill House near Faringdon and consisting of

30 *The 17th-century schoolhouse erected at Witney by Henry Box. This distinctive yet dignified building, dated 1660, reflected the architectural taste of the Commonwealth, its simple classicism in marked contract to the Baroque architecture favoured by the Royalists.*

Anno XV.

Caroli II. Regis.

An Act for the Setling of a Free-School in *Witney* in the County of *Oxon*, being Erected and Indowed by *Henry Box*, Citizen and Grocer of *London*, deceafed.

Whereas Henry Box, **Citizen and Grocer** of London lately deceaf= ed, hath out of a fincere inten= tion of publick good, at his own proper cofts and charges in his life time, Erected a large Free-School, with a very fair Houfe for one Schoolmafter and one Ufher, ftanding upon Two Acres of ground in Witney in the County of Oxon : And alfo by his Will in Writing declared his intention to fettle the faid Houfe and Two Acres of Land, and alfo Fifty pounds per Annum Rent=charge to be iffuing out of his Lands in the Parifh of Longworth in the County of Berks, then or now in the Occupa= tion of John Couldry or his Affigns, by Leafe for years, under the Rent of One hundred

A 2   and

31 *The title page of the Act for 'the Settling of a Free-School in Witney', passed by the 'Cavalier Parliament' in 1663.*

a large school room flanked by the master's and usher's houses.

At this juncture, external events intervened. Oliver Cromwell, the Lord Protector, had died (at the height of an apocalyptic thunder storm) on 3 September 1658. There was no obvious successor, and after a short and unhappy period of rule by Richard Cromwell (Oliver's son) the army intervened, Parliament was dissolved and Charles II returned as King on 25 April 1660. These momentous events took place while Henry Box was making arrangements for the foundation of his school, and it therefore became necessary to obtain an Act of Parliament to legalise the foundation. Henry Box died in 1662, but the Act of Incorporation was passed in the following year (15 Car.II cap.27).

The retrospective Act for the 'Settling of a Free-School in Witney in the County of Oxon' stipulated that the master and usher of the recently founded school would be Anglican ministers. The school's statutes reveal that the new place of learning would be:

> Free for the teaching of Latin, Greek and Hebrew, to thirty scholars, whereof such whose parents at the time of their birth inhabit the town of Witney (respect being had to the children of the poorest inhabitants) and founder's kin, should have priority; and if at any time such children should not amount to the number assigned, it should be lawful for the master, with the approbation of the visitors, to admit children that should be born of parents inhabiting within the town of Witney'.

The new school was endowed with an income of £50 per annum, arising from rent charges on Henry Box's properties 'in the manor of Worth, in the Parish of Longworth, in the County of Berkshire'. The first headmaster was Francis Gregory DD, who had been educated at Westminster and Trinity College, Cambridge.

In practice, the setting up of the school probably owed much to Mary Box (*née* Allen), Henry's second wife, who carried out her husband's wishes after his death. One senses that Mrs Box was a competent and well-educated woman, and in this context she would have been very much a product of the Commonwealth era, which had been in many ways a period of liberation for Englishwomen.

In accordance with his wishes, Henry Box was buried in St Mary's parish church, and his black marble memorial tablet can still be seen in the north transept. Freely translated, the Latin inscription tells us that Henry Box, gentlemen, was 'born in the year of our Lord 1585 and passed away in 1662' and that he founded a school in his native town with a 'large and elegant schoolhouse', containing accommodation for one headmaster and one assistant master. The memorial also explains that he spent his formative years at Oriel College, and later became a leading citizen of the City of London. The text pays due regard to Henry's pious nature, and concludes by mentioning that he had one son by his first wife and seven children by his second wife, Mary, who in an 'effusion of tears' had caused the memorial tablet to be erected.

The Population of 17th-Century Witney
Historians have at least two sources of information in relation to the population of towns such as Witney during the 17th century. These are the Protestation Returns of February 1641/2, and the Hearth Tax Returns of the 1660s. The Protestation Oath was taken by all adult males over the age of 18, and in some cases (e.g. Ducklington) the women, too, swore to maintain the Protestant religion along with their menfolk. Those who refused to swear – the Catholics – were listed as 'recusants'. Hence the returns show the names of all males over the age of 18, and it is an easy matter to calculate the adult population of a given town by multiplying by two.

In the case of Witney, we find that there were 650 adult males in the town in 1641, and this implies that there must have been about 1,300 adults of both sexes. Research has shown that about 40 per cent of the population of pre-industrial England was under 18 and in order to ascertain Witney's population in 1641, the approximate number of children – 520 – must be added to arrive at 1,820 as the total population. This is not, however, the final figure because the Witney return includes the names of those who lived in the hamlets of Hailey, Crawley and Curbridge but not those who lived in the parish of Cogges. This means that the populous part of Witney known as Newland does not figure in our total calculation, and we must therefore add the estimated population of Cogges (158 adults plus approximately 63 children equals 220) to the Witney total, and giving a grand total of 2,040 people living in or near Witney on the eve of the Civil War.

The Hearth Tax (a tax on fireplaces) was an easy tax to evade, as property-owners could block up their fireplaces when the tax was due, or simply lie to the 'Hearth Man'. The 1662 Hearth Tax Return lists 222 properties in Witney, Cogges and the surrounding hamlets, distributed as follows:

Witney	127 properties
Cogges	26 properties
Curbridge	30 properties
Crawley	10 properties
Hailey	29 properties

Most of these properties were single-hearth dwellings, although some houses were obviously much larger. Ralph Brideoake, for example, had 11 hearths in his rectory, while Robert Brice, in the old manor house, had nine. 'Widdow Crutchfield' paid tax on 12 hearths, and Lancellott Graunger admitted to as many as 15 hearths in his property.

To translate this data into a population figure we must apply a convenient multiplier based on the number of persons in a household. Gregory King, the 17th-century demographer, calculated that the average for urban communities was 4.45 persons, but later research has questioned this figure as extended families would have been common in semi-rural communities such as Witney. W.G. Hoskins suggests 6.5 as an average figure, and by multiplying 227 by 6.5, we arrive at a total of 1,443 inhabitants in Witney in the early 1660s.

The apparent decrease in population since 1641 may reflect economic disruption caused by the Civil War – or could it be that the inhabitants of Witney had become adept at avoiding a deeply unpopular tax?

5

Chapel and Industry

The Restoration was a curiously uneventful process and, in practice, many of the political changes made during the Interregnum were absorbed into the fabric of national life – the result being a move towards recognisably modern methods of government. Inevitably, however, there was a major shift in religious policy as Anglicans of the 'High Church' persuasion came flooding back into positions of power and responsibility, while the Bishop of Winchester's estates were restored, with the manor of Witney being leased to Sir Henry Hyde (later the Earl of Clarendon).

The Origins of Nonconformity
The 'Cavalier Parliament', which met on 8 May 1661 and sat for 18 years, was keen to restore the Church of England to its pre-war state. In pursuance of this aim, Parliament passed a series of Acts which were unacceptable to the more extreme Protestants. For example, all clergymen were required to make a public declaration of their assent and consent to the contents of the Prayer Book, while the supremacy of Parliament over the national church was clearly established. Ministers failing to comply with their revised terms of employment by 24 August 1662 were to be deprived of their livings.

In practice, the vast majority of clergymen conformed, and in Oxfordshire it is estimated that only 10 incumbents were 'ejected' in 1662, while 13 had already left in 1660. In other words, only 23 clergymen were ejected, and of these, four later decided to conform to the new order. The ejected ministers included William Gilbert, Witney's Puritan 'lecturer' at the very end of the Commonwealth period.

The events of 1662 were of seminal importance in that they changed the religious landscape in its entirety. Henceforth, there would no longer be just one national church to which all men and women belonged. Instead, there would be an established Church of England and a number of separate nonconformist sects. However, the legacy of the Reformation and the Civil War was a society which valued freedom of conscience; there

32   *Church Green, looking south towards St Mary's Church.*

33   *The Old Rectory, now known as Trelawney House, is situated immediately to the west of the parish church. This fine Georgian building was erected in 1723 by the Rev. Robert Freind and was one of the first houses in Witney to adopt the 'double-pile' plan in place of the simpler single-pile arrangement. The arms that can be seen above the doorway are those of Sir Jonathan Trelawny (1650-1721), the Bishop of Winchester, who in 1688 (when he was Bishop of Bristol) had been one of 'The Seven Bishops' who openly defied the Catholic King James II by refusing to read the Declaration of Indulgence from their pulpits.*

would be no more threats of inquisition or punishment, and although nonconformists were ejected from the positions of authority they were free to worship God in their own way and earn their livings from trade or business.

Old Dissent in Witney: the Quakers

In the case of Witney there were, at first, three forms of Protestantism – the Church of England, the Quakers, and the 'Independents'. The Quakers, or Society of Friends, are of considerable historic interest as an example of a Protestant sect that broke away from the national church before the upheavals of 1662. Witney's first Quaker meeting house was established in the 17th century, and a new building was erected at Woodgreen during the early 18th century, this characteristic structure being a single-storey Cotswold stone meeting house of the simplest kind.

In 1738, the Rev. Robert Freind (1684-1751), Witney's Anglican rector, stated that there were 30 families of Quakers within the town, and assuming that each of these families contained around five members, the Quaker population of Witney during the early 18th century would have been about one hundred and fifty. This number may appear modest, but the Quakers were always a minority sect, and in the context of Oxfordshire, 150 people would have constituted a significant body of dissenters.

The Witney Quakers were in decline by the later 18th century. The reasons for this decline can probably be explained by reference to the peculiar nature of many Quaker practices. Quakers of the old school were not allowed to marry out of the sect, while their children were accepted only when they had professed themselves to be 'enlightened'. In the 18th century, Quakers still wore the sombre garb of 17th-century Puritans, while 'pagan' words such as 'Friday' and 'March' were strictly forbidden.

These restrictions became repellent to many individual Quakers, and one can imagine younger 'Friends' rejecting their parents' religion, and going off to listen to local Independent minister. Later, when John Wesley began preaching in Witney, the incentives to leave the sect must have become overwhelming, and it is perhaps no coincidence that Witney's Quaker congregation shrank while the Wesleyans went from strength to strength. In later years, the Quakers adopted a more liberal attitude but, as far as Witney's Quakers were concerned, the damage seems to have been done, and this form of Old Dissent slowly withered away (albeit with a brief revival during the early 20th century).

Old Dissent: The Presbyterians and Independents

As far as can be ascertained, Witney's first nonconformist preacher was the Rev. John Dod, the former rector of Lower Heyford; in 1669 he was living in Witney and preaching at Cogges and elsewhere within Oxfordshire and Berkshire. Another early minister was the Reverenced Francis Hubert, the ejected vicar of Winterbourne Monkton, near Avebury in Wiltshire. The Reverenced Hubert was licensed to preach in Witney in 1672, and he is regarded as the town's first 'Independent' minister. Confusingly, Francis Hubert seems to

34 *The original Independent Chapel in Marlborough Lane was a starkly simple barn-like building with a steeply pitched gable roof. Its walls were of random rubble construction, while the door and window apertures were simple rectangular openings with traditional timber lintels. The entrance door was surmounted by a small window in the south gable. The red brick building visible to the left was a coach house associated with Batt House.*

have been a 'Presbyterian', and this underlines the fluid nature of nonconformist belief, the Independents being so loosely organised that it is hard to identify any specific doctrines, other than the independence of each congregation.

A charismatic preacher could, and often did, take an entire congregation on some private spiritual pilgrimage, and something of this nature appears to have happened in Witney. At one stage Witney had a Presbyterian congregation, while by 1781 the minister, Mr Mills, was said to have been a 'Baptist'. Later still, the Witney congregation joined the Association of Baptist Congregational Churches.

An Independent chapel was erected in Meeting House Lane in 1712, the first minister of this new place of worship being Samuel Mather, a nephew of Samuel Mather of Harvard University and the favourite preacher of Henry Cromwell when he was serving as Lord Deputy of Ireland. The chapel was a simple, barn-like building with a gabled roof. It was entirely devoid of decoration, although there were three memorial tablets to people who had been buried beneath the floor of the building. One of these tablets commemorated James Marriott (1743-1803), a blanket manufacturer who was nicknamed 'Little Active Jemmy' because of his squat stature and restless business energy. The presence of these memorials shows that Witney's 18th-century nonconformists were not by any means poor. Indeed, the Puritans and their descendants were often shrewd businessmen with a capacity for sustained hard work which made them wealthy men.

The size of the Independent congregation in Witney in 1715 was estimated at 'between 400 and 500', of whom about thirty were 'said to have been gentlemen, the rest tradesmen, farmers and labourers'. Later, in

35 *The new Independent chapel, opened in 1828, was basically a large hall with a raised gallery at the east end. Architectural treatment was concentrated on the High Street façade, which boasted a central door flanked by two tall windows and surmounted by a circular window with quatrefoil fenestration.*

1738, the Rev. Freind estimated that there were about 40 'Presbyterian, Independent and Anabaptist' families within the town In 1738; their preacher, Mr John Ward, was 'represented to be a Presbyterian'.

The number of worshippers declined towards the end of the 18th century, but in common with other nonconformist groups, the Independents experienced a revival during the social and political turmoil of the French Revolutionary wars. This revival continued into the 19th century, with the result that the Witney congregation decided to build themselves a new chapel. A site on the western side of Witney High Street was purchased for £700 in 1827, and the foundation stone was laid by Miss Townsend on 4 March 1828. The entire expense of the site and building was £2,000, of which no less than £1,200 was contributed by William Townsend of Witney.

The chapel was opened for public worship on 1 October 1828, the inaugural service being conducted by the Reverenced W. Jay of Bath, the Rev. J. Collison of Hackney and the Rev. Matthew Wilks of London. The new chapel was a large preaching hall with two windows on each side and a raised gallery at the east end. Architectural treatment was concentrated on this eastern façade, which faced the High Street and contained the main entrance. A central door was flanked by two tall windows in the usual chapel arrangement, the doorway being surmounted by a circular window with quatrefoil fenestration. The congregation faced westwards rather than east, and instead of a raised altar there was a pulpit for the minister. A range of Cotswold stone buildings at the rear of the chapel served as a manse and public rooms which were used for Sunday Schools and social gatherings.

New Dissent: Wesleyan Methodism in Witney

The Quakers, Baptists, Presbyterians and Independents are known, collectively, as the Old Dissenters because their religious beliefs harked back to the days of the Puritans. The Methodists, on the other had, are often described as 'New Dissenters', because their movement grew out of the teachings of John Wesley (1703-91) and his brother Charles.

John Wesley made numerous visits to Witney between 1764 and 1789, and his diary contains many references to the town. He found his congregations 'large and deeply attentive'; they were composed of 'such a people' as he had not seen, 'so remarkably diligent in business, and at the same time of so quiet a spirit, and so calm and civil in their behaviour'. This may hint that those who came to listen to the famous preacher were already committed Christians, in which case John Wesley would literally have been preaching to the converted. On one occasion, his sermon was accompanied by a violent thunderstorm of apocalyptic proportions, which must have greatly facilitated the work of the Lord!

Witney's Wesleyan Methodists erected their first chapel in the 1790s, the chosen site being on the east side of the High Street in the very centre of the town. The first meeting house was a two-storey Cotswold stone structure with a centrally placed west doorway and symmetrical Georgian-style window openings; the gable was graced by a circular window, and the words 'WESLEYAN CHAPEL' were prominently displayed across the front of the building.

36   *Witney's Wesleyan Methodists erected their first chapel in the 1790s, on the east side of the High Street in the very centre of the town. This first meeting house was a two-storey Cotswold stone structure with a centrally placed west doorway and symmetrical Georgian-style window openings. The gable was graced by a circular window, and the words 'WESLEYAN CHAPEL' were prominently displayed across the front of the building.*

New Dissent: The Primitive Methodists

The Primitive Methodists, a breakaway sect from the mainstream Wesleyan Methodists, were founded by Hugh Bourne, a Staffordshire millwright, during the early 19th century. It is unclear when Primitive Methodism first took root in Witney, although the Rev. William Allcock was preaching in the town in the early 1820s. In 1826 Witney became the head of a 'circuit', with the Rev. John Hallam as its preacher. A Primitive Methodist chapel is known to have been in existence within the town by 1845, and this became a Sunday School following the erection of a new chapel in 1869.

The Primitive Methodists were, arguably, more democratic than most of the other nonconformist groups, and they seem to have appealed particularly to working-class worshippers. As E.P. Thompson has suggested, Wesleyan Methodism often seemed to be a religion for the poor, whereas Primitive Methodism was a religion of the poor, the uncompromising preaching of the Primitives being 'as hard as the lives of their congregations'.

37   *The Primitive Methodist chapel erected in Corn Street in 1869 was, in many ways, similar to the Congregational chapel. The building was attractively built of local stone, with a low-pitched slated roof. The minister here in 1874 was the Rev. John Hill. In 1916 the Primitive Methodist minister was the Rev. R. Cowie, while Mrs Cowie ran the Primitive Sunday School. The building was used as a launderette during the 1960s, although the façade has latterly been restored.*

The Anglican Church

Notwithstanding the obvious strength of nonconformity in 18th- and early 19th century Witney, the majority of local people remained loyal to the Anglican Church. In 1738, the Rev. Robert Freind estimated that the population of Witney and the contiguous hamlets of Hailey, Crawley and Curbridge was 2,400, all of these people being 'tradesmen, inn-holders, farmers, day-labourers and the poor'. If, as he suggested, there were around 70 nonconformist families in the area, the combined dissenting population would have been about 350 – or around 15 per cent of the total population. The nonconformists were, moreover, divided between four or more competing sects, and as such they offered very little threat to the hegemony of the Anglican Church.

The church was, in every sense, a part of the establishment and a veritable tool of the ruling class. Many incumbents were members of the aristocracy or landed gentry, the church being a respectable career for the younger sons of landed families. Witney's rectors typically belonged to this leisured class, and like many incumbents during the 18th and 19th centuries they enjoyed private incomes far in excess of their clerical salaries. The Rev. Freind, for instance, was an absentee who claimed to spend five months of the year in Witney, but probably spent most of his time at Westminster School, where he was the headmaster.

The supposed laxness of the Church of England during the Georgian era has attracted much criticism (especially from nonconformist historians) but, as Elie Halevy has put it, 'a Church so secular, so deeply involved in what devout souls called the world, was not, it would seem, a Church to harbour fanatics'. On reflection, this makes the Church of England and its often deeply eccentric clergymen considerably more attractive than some of the more self-righteous chapel sects. Furthermore, as a national church, the Church of England was a wholly inclusive church, with special responsibility for the souls of the poor and dispossessed. These factors help to explain the continuing

38a and b *The Church of St Mary, Cogges. The religious census of 1851 revealed that, on the day of the census, Cogges Church was attended by 120 worshippers.*

adherence to the majority of Witney people to a church which, for all its imperfections, had struck deep roots in the national consciousness.

The Blanket Industry in the 18th Century

The Witney blanket industry was dominated by nonconformist families such as the Earlys, Colliers and Marriotts, most of whom were related to each other by birth or marriage. The master weavers served apprenticeships in their chosen trade, and this ensured that the leading manufacturers retained close links with their workers. Writing in the second half of the 17th century in his book *The Natural History of Oxfordshire*, Dr Robert Plot (1640-96) recorded that there were about sixty 'blanketers' within the town at that time. Between them, these small masters owned 'at least 150 looms, employing 3,000 poor people, from children to decrepit old age'. They worked 'about a hundred packs of wool per week', most of this being fell wool from slaughtered sheep.

In 1711, 'the blankett weavers inhabiting in and near Witney' obtained a charter of incorporation from Queen Anne to legally organise themselves into a guild or company for the better regulation of their industry. In 1721 the Company of Blanket Weavers erected a Baroque 'Blanket Hall' in Witney High Street as their headquarters at a total cost of £430, including £85 for the site, and this building remained in use until the 1840s. The charter, which is dated 23 May 1711, sets out the geographical limits of the Witney blanket-making area:

> Know ye, therefore, that wee of our especial grace ... have granted, constituted, declared, ordained, and appointed, and by these presents, for us, our heirs and successors, doe grant, constitute and declare, ordain and appoint, that all and every such persons, who are qualified by law as blankett weavers to use and exercise the art and mistery of blankett weaving in Witney aforesaid or twenty miles round the same, be incorporated by the name of The Master, Assistants, Wardens and Commonality of Blankett Weavers inhabiting in Witney, in the county of Oxon, or within twenty miles thereof.

The specified territorial limit of 20 miles around the town meant that (in theory at least) 'Witney' blankets could be made in a number of other places, including Oxford, Abingdon, Lambourn, Fairford, Northleach, Stow-on-the-Wold, Chipping Norton and Woodstock. In pre-industrial days, this definition made perfect sense as carding and spinning were still carried out on a domestic basis over a large area of the Cotswolds. Weaving, in contrast, took place in or near Witney, while fulling, which required adequate water power, was undertaken in mechanised fulling mills such as New Mill that had been in use since the Middle Ages.

The Company of Blanket Weavers was, as its name implied, a company of weavers who, in the pre-industrial period, obtained their yarn from domestic spinners and then wove it into blankets, tilts or other types of broad cloth. There were around sixty master weavers in Witney during the mid-18th century, all of whom were independent traders as opposed to the employees of larger organisations. In 1767, for example, the

39 *The Blanket Hall was built in 1721 at a total cost of £430 including £85 for the site. A relic of the Witney Blanket Weavers' Company, the building recalls 'pre-factory' organisation in Witney. In those days, every blanket made in the town was brought here for weighing and measuring. The one-handed clock high on the façade is of particular interest.*

Blanket-makers' Company had sixty members, employing perhaps 60 'journeymen' and 60 apprentices. Their handlooms were set up in houses or small workshops in various parts of the town, weaving mills being non-existent in Georgian Witney.

Blanket material was woven into lengths of cloth known as 'stockfulls'. The precise weight and length of each stockfull varied according to the type of blanket involved but, as an example, a 'six-quarter' blanket would contain 12 pairs (later 14) of blankets, each of which measured two yards in length and one-and-a-half yards in breadth. When the weaving process had been completed the material was handed over to the 'tuckers', who carried out the important finishing processes known as fulling, tentering and carding. The tuckers were at that time an entirely separate branch of the trade, who worked on their own premises and did not belong to the Company.

Fulling was originally accomplished by trampling the cloth in tubs or troughs, but by the medieval period human feet had been replaced by water-driven fulling stocks, fulling being the very first part of the textile industry to have been mechanised. Fulling mills normally incorporated two heavy wooden 'hammers', which were actuated by projecting cams or tappet systems on a revolving shaft. Each stockfull of cloth was immersed in a vat or trough filled with a type of clay known as 'fuller's earth' and thoroughly beaten by the fulling stocks, an important process as it removed all traces of natural wool-grease and also the oil that had been added to the wool prior to spinning.

When each stockfull had been thoroughly washed and scoured it was removed from the vat and taken to the tentering grounds for stretching and drying. This was achieved by affixing the wet cloth to wooden racks with the aid of 'tenter hooks' – a difficult operation when it is remembered that a typical stockfull might be 150ft long with a weight of about 100lbs when wet.

Some blanket names, weights and dimensions, c.1763 (after Plummer)

Name	Minimum Weight (per stockfull)	Pairs of Blankets (per stockfull)	Length of blanket	Width of blanket
Six Quarter Blankets	68lbs	14	2 yds	1.5 yds
Seven Quarter Blankets	68lbs	10	2.25 yds	1.75 yds
Eight Quarter Blankets	68lbs	8	2.25 yds	2 yds
Nine Quarter Blankets	68lbs	6	2.75 yds	2.25 yds
Ten Quarter Blankets	75lbs	5	3 yds	2.5 yds
Eleven Quarter Blankets	75lbs	4	3.25 yds	2.75 yds
Twelve Quarter Blankets	70lbs	3	3.5 yds	3 yds

The other process undertaken by the tuckers was raising the nap with the aid of teasel heads to produce the desired 'fluffy' texture of completed blanket cloth. This operation was sometimes performed mechanically by gig mills or 'rowing machines'.

Improved Transport Facilities

Late Georgian Witney was no longer a rural backwater; much of the medieval forest had been cleared away, and the primeval marshes had been drained and turned into good meadowland. Transport facilities had been greatly improved during the 18th and early 19th centuries, and local waterways were becoming increasingly important. It is known, for example, that a wharf had been established on the upper Thames at Eynsham, some five miles to the east, by the year 1312, when a 'hythe' is mentioned in a lease of Eynsham Abbey. The wharves at Eynsham, Newbridge and Radcot assumed a new importance in

40 *A stagecoach stands in front of the town hall, part of a 're-enactment' that took place during the inter-war years. The former* Crown Hotel *can be seen in the background.*

1789, when the Oxford Canal was linked to the Thames. In that same year, the Thames and Severn Canal was linked to the river at Lechlade, and the upper Thames was thereby transformed into an important east-to-west route.

Meanwhile, developments in road transport and road building had resulted in several local roads being improved and resurfaced. In 1766, for instance, a meeting held in the *Crown Hotel* at Witney resulted in an application being made to Parliament for powers to construct a turnpike road from Witney to the River Thames at Newbridge. The main road from Witney to Eynsham was improved and widened at about the same time, while the elegant toll bridge at Swinford was opened in 1769 to replace an earlier ferry.

These new roads and waterways formed part of a surprisingly comprehensive transport system which enabled coal and other heavy goods to be brought by boat to local wharves such as Eynsham or Newbridge and then conveyed by road transport the remaining few miles to Witney or to other destinations. Witney traders appear to have made good use of these improved road and river links. For example, Richard Parker, who described himself as a 'carrier and corn dealer', opened a coal wharf at Eynsham in 1827 and was soon one of the most important traders on the upper river; in 1829, we find him claiming the right of Free Navigation as far downstream as London.

The later 18th and early 19th centuries were not only the golden age of the waterways; they were also the heyday of the stagecoaches, and Witney, with a main road following its High Street and then turning a sharp right into Corn Street, became an important coaching centre. Long-distance road journeys could be made by a network of stagecoach services linking towns such as Woodstock, Witney and Burford with London, South Wales and other parts of the country, and by the end of the Napoleonic Wars about forty stagecoaches or mail coaches passed along the Oxford to Cheltenham road each day. Neighbouring Burford (which was sited at a crossroads) appears to have been more important as an interchange point, but Witney no doubt profited as a meal stop.

The *Marlborough* was one of the principal coaching inns in Witney, with extensive stabling accommodation at the rear. In 1823, at the height of the stagecoach era, an 'up' mail coach left here every day at 9.30 a.m. sharp, while a 'down' coach passed through at 4.30 p.m. en route for Cheltenham. Other coaches left from the *Kings Arms*, the *Staple Hall* and the *Crown*, while another twenty or so smaller inns, taverns and beer shops catered for the needs of humbler travellers.

West Oxfordshire had reached a high level of development by the end of the 18th century. Its people were well clothed and well fed, they lived in solid stone houses, and their methods of production were becoming ever more sophisticated. Economic growth was probably running at between two and three per cent per annum, capital was accumulating, and technological innovation was an accepted feature of the local textile industry. Flying shuttles and power spinning, for example, appear to have been introduced in Witney by about 1800, the first water-powered spinning equipment having been installed in New Mill. The population of Witney and its satellite hamlets was approximately 4,500 by that time.

The Napoleonic War

The great war waged against Revolutionary and Napoleonic France had little obvious effect on West Oxfordshire, although Wychwood Forest is said to have provided timber for Nelson's warships. In retrospect, the protracted French wars presented unprecedented opportunities for Witney manufacturers, who found a ready and lucrative market for products such as blankets, mops and hammocks. Writing in 1814, John Harris stated that the war had furnished the weavers with employment, blankets being 'wanted in great numbers for the use of the various armaments sent on foreign expeditions'.

In view of the more or less guaranteed markets for army and navy blankets, it is perhaps no coincidence that power spinning and other technical innovations should have been introduced at Witney during the Napoleonic period. In 1809, Arthur Young, in his *General View of the Agriculture of Oxfordshire*, suggested that machinery was earning £4,000 per annum, and Witney was flourishing, though there was great distress among the former hand spinners in surrounding villages whose livelihood had been destroyed by the new machines.

Witney was too far inland for men to be 'pressed' for service in the Navy, and in any case untrained landsmen were of little use on an active warship. On the other hand, local men served in the army during the long years of conflict with France. One of these soldiers was Patrick William Moulder of the 15th, or King's, Regiment of Hussars, who had witnessed the death of Sir John Moore at the Battle of Corunna and had participated in the battles of Vittoria, the Pyrenees, Orthes and Toulouse before taking part in the Battle of Waterloo on 18 June 1815.

In later years Patrick Moulder, who was also landlord of the *Cross Keys* inn, became Regimental Sergeant-Major of the Oxfordshire Yeomanry Cavalry under the command of the Right Hon. Lord Churchill. Sadly, Sergeant-Major Moulder took his own life in December 1838. It was reported that he had removed a pistol from the yeomanry storeroom on the upper floor of the inn, gone down to an outhouse in the yard, and put a bullet in his brain; his servant found him with 'his head shot to atoms'.

41 *The* Cross Keys *inn in 1828, as shown in a painting by S. Jones. The cart entrance visible to the left of the building gave access to the 'close behind the inn' in which Sergeant-Major Moulder shot himself.*

It was revealed at the subsequent inquest that the local surgeon, Dr Edward Batt (1801-52), had been attending the deceased for 'some time past' and that he 'had a disease of the heart which generally produced great effect on the mind and depressed the spirit'. Notwithstanding the manner of his death, Sergeant-Major Moulder was buried with full military honours in the churchyard of St Mary's parish church at Witney on 18 December 1838. The funeral must have been one of the largest ever seen at Witney, with around 3,000 people gathering to pay their respects to this Waterloo veteran.

6

The Age of Steam

The end of the Napoleonic War in 1815 was followed by a period of rising prosperity and unprecedented material progress. Though there were harvest failures and economic problems during the 1840s, in general the 19th century was a period of great opportunities for those engaged in trade or industry. Perhaps for the first time in history, men and women believed that progress was an inevitable process and that, moreover, individual people could strive for and achieve success in any field of human endeavour. In consequence, the Victorian era was a period of rapid and unprecedented change in which Witney was transformed. In particular, the construction of the railway represented a feat of engineering that far exceeded anything that had gone before.

Some Early Railway Schemes

The first plans for a railway through Witney were made as early as 1836, when the London and Birmingham Railway promoted a line from Tring, through Oxford and Witney, to Cheltenham. This line, which would have been built to what later became the standard gauge of 4ft 8½in, was rejected by Parliament in favour of the broad-gauge (seven-foot) Cheltenham and Great Western Union Railway, which joined the Great Western Railway main line at Swindon.

A spate of schemes came during 'The Railway Mania' years of the 1840s, the first in the field being 'The Oxford, Witney, Cheltenham and Gloucester Independent Railway', which obtained an Act of Parliament for the construction of a 'mixed' (i.e., dual) gauge line from Oxford to Cheltenham. The GWR and its ally the Oxford Worcester and Wolverhampton Railway (later the West Midland) then obtained powers for a branch line to Witney via North Leigh, while the standard-gauge faction resurrected their earlier scheme for a line from Tring to Cheltenham. Other railways were projected at that time, but few can have been serious attempts to build new railways. In particular, it seems that the Great Western schemes were 'bluffs' designed to keep rival companies away from the Oxford and Cheltenham areas.

It appeared that Witney was destined to become a rural backwater, isolated from the railway network and thereby cut off from the mainstream of Victorian economic development. Writing in the early 1850s, the local historian Dr J.A. Giles commented on a 'partial gloom' which seemed to hang over the town at that time. This was due, not just to the lack of rail communication, but also to the decline of the stagecoaches on the Oxford to Cheltenham Road. 'Three coaches per day', he recorded, 'are now the melancholy survivors of the incessant swarm which once added life to the streets of Witney, and put money into the pockets of its numerous horse-keepers, publicans and stable boys.'

Formation of the Witney Railway Company

Happily, Witney was saved from the fate of towns such as Northleach and Burford by an unexpected occurrence. Relations between the Oxford, Worcester and Wolverhampton Railway and the parent Great Western company had been severely strained for some time, mainly because the Banbury to Birmingham line had been adopted as the main GWR route to the North. The OW&WR directors felt that this was a breach of faith, and began negotiations with the standard-gauge companies. By 1854, standard gauge trains were running from Worcester to Euston via the Yarnton Loop, a short connecting line to the north of Oxford.

This was good news for the inhabitants of Witney, as it meant that there was now a chance of their rail link being built. Indeed, in the previous year, the OW&WR had sought powers for a line between Yarnton, Witney and Cheltenham. The Bill had been thrown out, but it nevertheless suggested to the promoters of the Witney Railway that powerful main line interests would support them should they decide to present a more modest scheme to Parliament.

As the first step towards implementing their scheme, the leading supporters of the venture held a public meeting in Witney on

ANNO VICESIMO SECUNDO & VICESIMO TERTIO

VICTORIÆ REGINÆ.

****

Cap. xlvi.

An Act for connecting the Town of *Witney* with the existing Railways in the Parishes of *Yarnton* and *Wolvercot* in the County of *Oxford;* and for other Purposes.   [1st *August* 1859.]

WHEREAS the making of a Railway from the Town of *Witney* to a Point near the Parish Boundary of *Cassington* and *Yarnton*, with a Railway therefrom to afford Access to the existing Railways in the Parishes of *Yarnton* and *Wolvercot* in the County of *Oxford*, would be of public Advantage: And whereas the Persons in that Behalf named in this Act, and others, are willing to make and maintain the Railways by this Act authorized, and it is expedient that they be incorporated with proper Powers and Provisions for that Purpose: And whereas the Objects of this Act cannot be attained without the Authority of Parliament: May it therefore please Your Majesty that it may be enacted; and be it enacted by the Queen's most Excellent Majesty, by and with the Advice and Consent of the Lords Spiritual and Temporal, and Commons, in this present Parliament assembled, and by the Authority of the same, as follows; (to wit,)

I. This Act may be cited for all Purposes as "The *Witney* Railway Short Title. Act, 1859."

II. The "Companies Clauses Consolidation Act, 1845," the "Lands 8 & 9 Vict. Clauses Consolidation Act, 1845," and the "Railways Clauses Conso- cc. 16. 18. & lidation Act, 1845," save so far as any of the Clauses and Provisions of porated. those

[*Local.*]   7 K

42 *The title page of the Witney Railway Act of Incorporation.*

43   Charles Early (1824-1912), the proprietor of Witney Mill and a long-serving director of the Witney Railway Company.

23 December 1858. Around 400 people turned up, and it soon became clear that the people of the locality had lost all patience with the Great Western and other main line companies which had, for many years, done little more than talk about a railway between Oxford and Witney. The meeting enthusiastically decided to form a company in order to build a branch line from Witney to the Oxford, Worcester and Wolverhampton railway at Yarnton, and a provisional committee, led by John Williams Clinch, James Clinch, Charles Clinch, Augustine Batt, Joseph Druce, John Pickering and William Furlonge, set about raising capital for the new project.

The committee engaged Sir Charles Fox (1810-74), a well-known Victorian engineer, to survey the route and prepare the necessary plans and sections, and in November 1858 the promoters gave formal notice that they intended to make an application to Parliament in the ensuing session for 'An Act to Incorporate a Company for Making and Maintaining a Railway from Witney to Yarnton, in the County of Oxford', with 'all necessary stations, works, and conveniences connected therewith'.

The Witney Railway Bill went before Parliament in the following year. The Great Western fought the Bill vigorously, but the Witney Company had the support of the rival standard-gauge companies, and the scheme received the Royal Assent on 1 August 1859. The resulting Act of Parliament (22 and 23 Vic. cap.46) provided consent for the construction of a railway from Witney to Yarnton, a distance of 8 miles 13 chains. With meticulous accuracy, the authorised route was treated as two separate lines which, for convenience, were described as 'Railway Number One' and 'Railway Number Two'. Railway Number One, the main part of the line, was defined as:

44   Malachi Bartlett (1802-75), the founder of a well-known Witney building firm, was a supporter of the railway and was engaged by the railway company to complete the stations and other works. The Witney builder thereby became involved in a whole range of tasks, including track-laying, fencing, sign-writing, painting and road-construction. He was also awarded several smaller contracts, for the construction of a 'tank house' and other works, at Witney.

A railway commencing at or near the north-west corner of an arable field occupied by Thomas Shuffrey, and abutting westerly on Pound Lane, and northerly on the grounds belonging to the Mount or Old Manor House, all in Curbridge in the Parish of Witney and County of Oxford, and terminating at the fence or ditch being the boundary between the parishes of Cassington and Yarnton, in the said County of Oxford, at a distance of thirty-three chains, measured along such boundary southwards, from the road leading from Cassington to Yarnton.

A time limit of four years was set for completion of the works, while the authorised capital was £50,000 in £10 shares, with a further £16,000 by loans. Walter Strickland, Charles Early, Henry Akers, George Hewitt the younger, John Williams Clinch, Joseph Druce, William Holland Furlonge and Charles Locock Webb were mentioned by name as the first directors, and these gentlemen were to continue in office until the first ordinary meeting of the company, at which meeting 'the shareholders present, personally or by proxy, would elect a new body of directors, or allow the original directors to continue in office'.

Construction of the Line

Construction of the single-line branch started at Eynsham in May 1860 and, with few physical obstacles to hinder the navvies, rapid progress was made. At the half-yearly meeting in March 1861, Sir Charles Fox was able to report that the heaviest works were nearing completion and five miles of the route were ready to receive the permanent way. Already, he added, 450 tons of rails had been delivered in readiness for the track-laying. On 10 August 1861, the directors announced that the line was in so forward a state that they had that very morning been able to travel over the whole of it on a locomotive. Having passed its Board of Trade Inspection on 5 November, the new railway was officially opened on Wednesday 13 November 1861.

The opening of the railway was treated as a public holiday in Witney, and the whole town was decorated with flags and bunting. The mill workers and school children were given a holiday, and the latter were marched down to the station and given buns and oranges to eat. Ignoring the November rain,

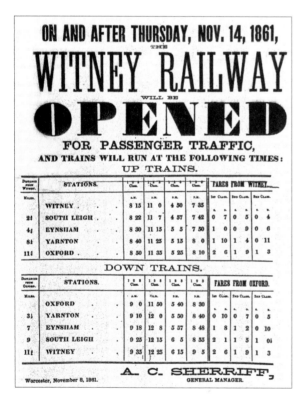

45 *A time-bill showing the original Witney Railway timetable – the 35-minute journey time between Witney and Oxford being considerably quicker than present-day journeys on congested roads.*

46 *Opened on 13 November 1861, Witney's first station was a small single platform terminus near the parish church. The little station had a life of just under 12 years until, on 15 January 1873, it was replaced by a new station on the East Gloucestershire Railway's Fairford extension. The original Witney Railway terminus was then given over entirely to goods traffic, and the old timber-framed station building became a goods office.*

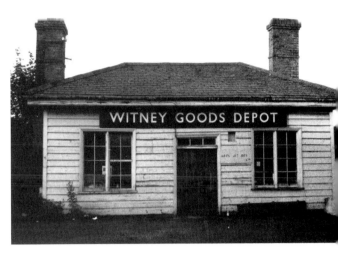

many hundreds of people made their way across Church Green to the station and by mid-day vast crowds were milling about on the platform and in Station Lane, a new road made by the railway company to create a better means of access to the terminus.

The official first train arrived around mid-morning and, as the gleaming green West Midland locomotive came to rest in the shadow of St Mary's church, it was greeted by cheers and waving flags; bells rang out from the church tower, and the band of the Volunteer Rifle Corps played martial airs. The first 'up' train from Witney to Oxford left at 11.00 a.m., 'amid the hearty cheering of the spectators', while the band played a 'lively tune'. The train consisted of about 14 short-wheelbase coaches, most of which were well filled with enthusiastic first-day travellers. At 1.00 p.m. the branch train started back from Oxford, 'where a large accession of passengers, who had been invited by the directors, availed themselves of the return trip to Witney'.

Later, a sheep was roasted whole in the market place for the artisans and labouring classes, while the directors sat down to entertain the local gentry in St Mary's School, where a 'very elegant *déjeuner*' had been provided. According to *Jackson's Oxford Journal*:

47 *Rear and end elevations of the 1861 station building, showing the canopy, which was later boxed-in to form a store-room. The extensions contained urinals and what may have been a porters' room.*

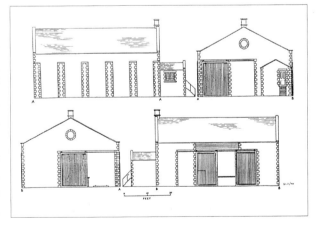

48 *Plans of the substantial, Cotswold stone goods shed, which was brought into use in 1862 when a full freight service was introduced on the Witney railway.*

The company at once proceeded there, and lost no time in securing places at the table. The room was tastefully decorated, and on the wall at the back of the Chairman's seat was executed, in flowers and evergreens, SUCCESS TO THE WITNEY RAILWAY. The déjeuner, which was provided by Mr Gillett, of the *Marlborough Arms*, was distinguished for its excellence and abundance, and was accompanied by champagne, moselle, and hock *ad libitum*.

The entertainment reflected equal credit on the liberality of the directors and on the taste and judgement displayed by Mr Gillett. Upwards of 200 persons, including a large number of ladies, partook of the déjeuner, and there was a general expression of approbation at the manner in which every thing was arranged for the comfort and enjoyment of the largest festive party that has ever assembled in the good old town of Witney.

Several speeches were made after the dinner, notably by the chairman of the company, who proposed toasts to the Queen, the royal family, the army, the navy and the volunteers, while the Rifles Band played the national anthem. After Mr Strickland had finished, he was followed (among others) by Captain Fane, Ensign Clinch, Sir Charles Fox, Edward Early and the Rev. Richard Sankey.

Regular train services commenced on the following day, with eastbound, or 'up' departures from Witney at 08.15 a.m., 11.00 a.m., 4.50 p.m. and 7.35 p.m., and balancing 'down' workings from Oxford at 9.00 a.m., 11.50 a.m., 5.40 p.m. and 8.30 p.m. The through fares to Oxford were 2s. 6d. first class, 1s. 9d. second class and ls. 3d. for third class. Intermediate stations were provided at Eynsham and South Leigh, and trains reached Oxford in 35 minutes (later reduced to half an hour). The Witney railway owned no locomotives or rolling stock of its own. Instead, the line was worked by the West Midland Railway under the terms of an operating agreement.

As a short feeder branch, the Witney railway was fairly successful. Full goods facilities were introduced on 1 March 1862 and the railway was soon carrying an inwards traffic of coal and wool and an outwards traffic of blankets. Gross receipts amounted to £2,237 in the first half of 1863 and, after 50 per cent had been deducted to pay the West Midland Railway for working the line, the directors were able to recommend a dividend of 2½ per cent on ordinary capital and five per cent on preference shares. In that same year, the West Midland Railway was amalgamated with the GWR and, thereafter, all services on the Witney railway were worked by the Great Western company.

Extension to Fairford

Although the Witney railway had been opened as a purely local route, the directors were anxious to extend their branch line beyond Witney, and in 1859 the company asked its engineer to survey an extension to Northleach, at which point it was hoped to form a connection with a line from Cirencester. In the event, the Witney railway never progressed beyond Witney, and any extension plans which might have existed in the minds of the directors were drastically revised when the East Gloucestershire Railway (EGR) burst upon the scene.

49 *Witney Goods Junction marked the physical boundary between the 1861 Witney Railway and the East Gloucestershire Railway of 1873, the right-hand spur being the original 'main line' into Witney terminus, while the left-hand line was the EGR route to Bampton and Fairford. The siding on the extreme right was used as a 'head-shunt' for the goods yard.*

The East Gloucestershire Railway was born at a meeting held at Hatherop Castle, near Fairford, in 1861. This meeting was attended by the squires and landowners of East Gloucestershire and West Oxfordshire and 'the whole gentry of the county ... who had for many years been trying to get the railway'. The line concerned was to run from Cheltenham to Andoversford and thence southwards along the Coln Valley to Lechlade. Here the line would divide, with one arm heading eastwards to join the Witney railway, while the other would run southwards to form a junction with the Faringdon railway.

A slightly modified scheme was sanctioned by Parliament on 7 August 1862 (25 and 26 Vic.cap.10) but, before construction could begin, a group of Great Western shareholders suddenly decided that the East Gloucestershire scheme was an unnecessary and risky proposition. Eventually, so many shareholders joined the campaign that the Great Western was obliged to withdraw its support. Undeterred, the supporters of the EGR formed a new alliance with the rival Midland Railway and, in open defiance of the GWR, a new Bill was submitted to Parliament in the 1864 session.

50 *A c.1912 postcard view of Witney passenger station, which replaced the earlier station in 1873. A 'Metro' class 2-4-0 side tank locomotive has just arrived with a westbound train, which has disgorged its passengers on the down platform. The low-roofed vehicle behind the locomotive is a slat-sided 'Siphon', for conveying milk churns.*

51 *A postcard view of c.1911, showing the 1873 passenger station. The roof of the 'down'-side waiting shelter can be seen to the left, while the signal box is sited on the platform to the right of the Cotswold stone station building.*

The Bill was examined at great length by a Select Committee of the House of Commons, and at even greater length by a Lords Committee. Several witnesses were called to give evidence, including Walter Strickland and Charles Early. Mr Strickland, the Witney railway chairman, declared that the Witney line had always been considered 'the first link in a railway to Cheltenham', but plans for an extension to Lechlade had been abandoned following the failure of the 1862 East Gloucestershire proposals.

Charles Early, the Witney blanket manufacturer, stated that in his opinion the Witney railway had been an 'immense advantage to Witney as a manufacturing town'. His mills and workshops consumed considerable amounts of wool, oil and coal, although

52 *Members of the station staff pose on the 'up' platform, while a former main line 2-2-2 locomotive poses for the camera. Great Western engines were painted mid-green with highly polished brasswork.*

53 (Above) A 'Sir Alexander' class 2–2–2 locomotive stands in Witney goods yard at the head of a blanket special in 1911. The tall chimney of Mount Mill can be seen in the background.

54 (Left) Signalman 'Cis' Bustin poses with the crew of '1854' class 0–6–0 saddle tank locomotive No. 1858, photographed at Witney around 1920.

55 Most of the Witney station staff appear in this group photograph taken outside the old station building in the 1920s. Those present include (back row left to right) F. Wilson, S. Franklin, T. Turner. C. Bustin, A. Townsend, J. Robinson, J. Simpson; (centre row) R. Webb, C. Ayres, W. Wyatt, G. Sherbourne, J. Hicks, J. Alderman; (front row) C. Farmer, E. Lowe, stationmaster J. Pugh, G. Wilkins and F. Law; the gentleman on the extreme right is unknown.

56 *A Great Western horse-dray, piled high with Witney blankets, heads towards the station. The drayman is Mr Humphreys.*

very little coal came from South Wales because of the lack of a suitable rail link between West Oxfordshire and the Welsh coal fields; however, he thought that this situation would change if the EGR line was built. He added that several carriers' carts came into Witney every day and 'ran up to the station', but the stagecoaches that had formerly provided a service between London, Witney and Cheltenham had all been 'taken off the road'.

The Bill was finally passed by Parliament on 29 July 1864, when the revised East Gloucestershire scheme received the Royal Assent (27 and 28 Vic.cap 285). The East Gloucestershire Railway Company was thereby empowered to build a railway from Cheltenham to Faringdon with a branch from Lechlade to Witney. Construction began at the western end of the route and, by the autumn of 1865, a tunnel and its associated earthworks were taking shape in the Gloucestershire countryside near Andoversford.

Although it was reported that 'considerable progress' had been made, it soon became evident that the company was unable to finance its entire scheme, and it was therefore decided that the EGR would concentrate its efforts on the completion of a 14 mile 10 chain branch between Witney and Fairford. As this short section of the original EGR scheme would traverse an almost dead-level tract of countryside, there would be no tunnels, few real cuttings and only one modest embankment at Curbridge.

The EGR company obtained an extension of time to complete the works in 1867, and in 1869 construction resumed on the Witney to Fairford section. The line was ceremonially opened on 14 January 1873 when what must have been the first down train arrived in Fairford as an 'empty stock working', but otherwise the main celebrations took place on Wednesday 15 January in connection with the start of regular public services.

The day's events were fully recorded in the local press, and on Thursday 23 January 1873 the *Witney Express* reported that the first train had left Fairford at 7.30 a.m. carrying the directors and their invited guests. The engine was 'gaily adorned with flags and evergreens, and a large concourse of people assembled at the several stations to witness the arrival and departure of the trains on this new and capitally-constructed line'.

All the other trains run during the day were crowded, and a number of Fairford school children, both boys and girls, were 'by the kindness of J.R. Raymond Barker' provided with a luncheon 'and treated to a trip to Witney'. Elsewhere in the same issue, the *Witney Express* reported that there had been great rejoicing in Lechlade, while in the evening the town had

57 *A general view of Witney passenger station, looking east towards Oxford during the early 1960s. The barrow crossing in the foreground provided a means of access to the down platform.*

58 *The interior of the ticket office at Witney passenger station, c.1962. Staff present include Miss Davies and Mr Jones (standing at the rear). Confusingly, it is believed that the gentleman in the foreground was also called Mr Jones.*

59 *Witney passenger station, glimpsed from the cab of '57XX' class 0-6-0 pannier tank No. 9773 on Friday 31 December 1965, the last day of steam operation on the Witney railway.*

60 *Class '22' diesel–hydraulic locomotive No. D6332 draws slowly forwards into Witney old station in order to collect a wagon-load of industrial waste. The original 1861 platform can be seen to the right.*

61 *Class '22' locomotive No. D6328 runs round its train in Witney goods yard on 13 February 1968. Having been coupled to the rear of the incoming train, the engine will position the loaded wagons in the coal sidings and re-marshal its train before returning to Oxford.*

63   *Class '22' locomotive No. D6326 hurries a lengthy train of open wagons through the arch of the Stanton Harcourt road bridge, as it nears Witney with a 'down' freight train in the summer of 1970.*

been visited by the bandsmen of the Witney Temperance Society, who had arrived by train and marched through the streets.

Regular operations commenced on the following day, and the East Gloucestershire line then became an extension of the earlier Witney railway, with four trains each way between Oxford and Fairford. The two local railways thereby formed a single 22-mile branch, although all services ran over the main line to and from Oxford, a total distance of 25 miles 42 chains. Journeys between Oxford, Witney and Fairford were accomplished within one hour and 10 minutes.

As a result of this extension, the original Witney Railway terminus was closed to passengers, and a new station was opened at the bottom of the Church Leys. Thereafter, the 1861 station was adapted for use as a goods yard, in which capacity it remained in operation until November 1970.

Some Effects of the Railway

The railway enabled coal, wool and other commodities to be brought into Witney, with obvious advantages for mill owners such as Charles Early and William Smith. Steam-power began to supplement water power, Witney's first purpose-built steam mill being opened by William Smith in 1866. The railways also provided cheap and efficient transport for blankets and other products of the local factories, and by the early 1900s Witney station was handling around forty thousand tons of freight traffic a year, roughly 38 per cent of

62   *Class '22' locomotive No. D6348 carries out shunting operations in Witney goods yard, with the seven-ton yard crane visible to the left and the former GWR stables visible to the right of the picture.*

64 *On 5 December 1872 the* Witney Express *reported that a 'new footpath had been laid across the Leys', with young trees planted on either side, 'following a suggestion by Dr Batt'. The new path, known as Batt's Walk, provided a means of access to the 1873 station, thereby obviating a lengthy detour that would otherwise have been necessary around the perimeter of the Leys.*

this tonnage being in the form of inwards coal. In 1905, for example, the station handled 42,404 tons of freight traffic, including 16,183 tons of coal.

The GWR continued to operate the Oxford, Witney and Fairford line on behalf of the local companies until 1890, when it purchased the branch outright. Having obtained full possession of the line, the Great Western made many improvements, and Witney station eventually developed into a relatively busy branch line centre employing around 27 men and handling upwards of 40,000 tons of freight a year. In 1903, goods traffic amounted to 40,935 tons, rising to 46,652 tons in 1913. In that same year, the station dealt with 46,652 parcels, while 38,225 tickets were issued.

Traffic dealt with at Witney Station

Year	Staff	Receipts (£)	Tickets	Parcels	Goods Tonnage
1903	14	24,334	36,841	28,309	40,935
1913	21	27,552	38,225	46,652	43,762
1923	26	49,291	41,138	81,823	45,281
1929	25	40,346	17,834	97,440	40,869
1931	25	41,488	12,448	120,446	48,910
1933	26	36,094	19,359	95,804	49,059
1935	27	34,379	21,739	91,486	47,881
1936	27	33,763	22,458	77,621	50,031
1937	27	30,704	23,660	72,277	47,624
1938	27	30,936	20,643	74,752	40,701

65 *A panoramic view of Witney Old Station in November 1970, with the original Witney Railway terminus prominent to the right and the goods shed in the distance. The photograph was taken from the Mount Mill loading bay.*

7

The Witney Blanket Mills

The Windrush is the fastest-flowing river in Oxfordshire and, as such, it was the only river in the county suitable for powering textile mills. Writing in 1852, Dr J.A. Giles mentioned that, in a distance of 20 miles, 'the Windrush turns more than 20 mills, some used for grinding corn, and others for fulling the blankets and spinning the wool for the factories at Witney'. There were, he said, 'six thriving establishments' in the town at that time, consuming 120 packs of wool each week, each pack weighing 240 pounds; he estimated that the local industry was producing around 93,000 pairs of blankets each year, while the number of people employed in the trade was 'upwards of eight hundred, comprising men, women and children'. All of these individuals were 'employed on the premises of their masters', the old system of domestic manufacture having 'been upset by the introduction of machinery about forty years ago'.

Following the industrial revolution, blanket production had become more centralised, the spinning process being transformed by the introduction of water-powered spinning machinery in mills such as New Mill and Crawley Mill. The continued use of water power nevertheless ensured that Witney's spinning and fulling mills were spread out along the Windrush valley at intervals of about one mile – otherwise the power source would have been dissipated. For this reason, rural mills such as those at Worsham, Minster Lovell, Crawley and New Mill were still required and, indeed, some of them remained in use long after the introduction of steam power.

The main firms in operation during the 1850s were John Early and Co. (New Mill and Witney Mill); Richard Early (Witney Mill); Edward Early (New Mill and Farm Mill); Horatio Collier (Crawley Mill and Corn Street Mill); Edward Early Junior (Worsham Mill); and Early Brothers, who were operating from the former Blanket Hall, which had been sold the Earlys' company in 1844 for the sum of £200. There was in addition a 'tilting and yarn' factory at Woodgreen, owned by Richard Early Junior.

Full mechanisation of all branches of the Witney blanket industry was not achieved until the end of the Victorian period. By 1902 there were six steam-powered mills in operation, divided between four blanket-making firms as follows: Charles Early and Co. (New Mill and Witney Mill); William Smith and Co. (Crawley Mill and Bridge Street Mill); James Marriott and Sons (Mount Mill), and Messrs Pritchett and Webley (Worsham Mill). The last mentioned firm also had interests in a glove factory in Newland, and when Pritchett and Webley failed, the gloving side of the business carried on as a separate concern. The three remaining Witney blanket firms were operating about five hundred power looms by 1914.

Worsham Mill

This three-storey stone-built spinning mill, situated about four miles to the west of Witney, passed through the hands of several different owners during the 19th and 20th centuries. In 1852 it was being used by Richard Early, but it was then sold to his son (also called Richard) before passing into the hands of Arthur Early. Sadly, Arthur was committed to a lunatic asylum shortly afterwards, and in consequence the mill was leased to his relative Henry Early. In 1890 it was transferred to Messrs Pritchett and Webley, who erected new buildings and installed a water turbine and gas engine. The re-equipped mill provided facilities for all stages of blanket production from spinning to fulling and the finishing processes. At its peak the Worsham site provided work for around fifty looms, but the venture never prospered and Pritchett and Webley were eventually forced to close their business. After many vicissitudes, the mill passed into the hands of James Marriott and Sons.

Crawley Mill

Crawley Mill, situated about three miles downstream from Worsham, was used for blanket-making by the Collier family. It was later owned by Smith's Blankets, who used the site for fulling, bleaching, dyeing and other operations. The oldest part of the mill, dating from

66 *Crawley Mill was attractively situated in rural surroundings in the Windrush Valley, as shown in this early 20th-century photograph.*

67 *(Below) An aerial view showing a more modern part of Crawley Mill. These brick-built buildings were sited immediately to the south of the earlier water-powered mill.*

68 *A ground plan of Crawley Mill, showing the original mill to the north and the later buildings to the south. The long, thin structures were sulphur bleaching sheds.*

the 18th century, was a two-storey Cotswold stone structure, and like most of the older Witney mills it was built across the mill race, with the undershot wheel fully enclosed. A small, square chimney stack at the rear suggested that water power was assisted by an auxiliary steam engine from about 1860 onwards. The building was entirely traditional in construction and appearance, having thick load-bearing walls and timber beams, upon which the upper floor was supported.

A later mill, situated to the south of the original Cotswold stone building, was of red brick construction, and powered by steam, its cylindrical brick chimney stack a notable landmark in the otherwise rural surroundings of the Windrush Valley. An accretion of single-storey wooden bleach sheds near the road was used until the 1960s for sulphur bleaching, sulphuric acid having been used for bleaching in the late 18th century, although it did not immediately replace the earlier plant alkaline solutions.

New Mill

New Mill was, perversely, one of the oldest mills in Witney. Mechanised spinning machinery was first installed in the mill around 1790, and this innovation, which threw many hand

69 *A 1990s view of New Mill from the south-west.*

spinners out of work, marked the beginning of the Industrial Revolution in Witney. Sadly, Edmund Wright, who had installed the new machinery, later fell into the mill pond at New Mill and was crushed by his own water wheel, much to the delight of the redundant hand spinners!

The New Mill site was for many years used by the Early family, though it should be stressed that the owners of a particular mill or workshop were not necessarily the operators. New Mill, for example, was leased by a partnership of Edward Early, John Early and Paul Harris during the early 19th century, and these three partners carried out spinning for their own needs and for other firms. Shared ownership persisted at New Mill for many years, and in the 1880s the premises were being used by Charles Early (1824-1912), and his relatives Messrs Thomas and Walter Early.

Fire was a source of particular danger during the 18th and early 19th centuries. Houses and workshops were lit by rush lights, candles or oil lamps, which could easily be knocked over, and once fires had started they spread rapidly through closely spaced buildings. The introduction of gas lighting and steam power presented further problems, even though boilers and furnaces were often housed in detached buildings to reduce the risk of fire.

Despite these precautions, mill fires took place with considerable frequency. New Mill, for example, caught fire in 1783, 1809, 1818, and again in 1883. The premises were rebuilt after each disaster and by the 1880s the mill consisted of a large three-storey block sited at right angles to the river, containing carding, spinning and willeying equipment together with two breast-shot water wheels developing up to 60 horse power. Two extensions, on each side of the head race, contained fulling stocks and further spinning and carding machinery. A particularly spectacular fire took place at New Mill on 19 January 1883. It was, claimed the *Witney Gazette*,

> One of the most calamitous conflagrations that has ever taken place in the district ... the good people of our quiet town were about to retire to rest, when suddenly there burst upon the stillness of the night that most alarming cry of Fire! And when, in reply to enquiries, it was reported that New Mills were on fire, the consternation was very great. The night sky was lit up for miles around, and large numbers of people were soon hurrying down to the river to see 'the grand, but awful spectacle'.

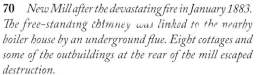

70   New Mill after the devastating fire in January 1883. The free-standing chimney was linked to the nearby boiler house by an underground flue. Eight cottages and some of the outbuildings at the rear of the mill escaped destruction.

71   Another view of New Mill after the disastrous fire in 1883. The rear parts of the building suffered major damage, although the tucking shops and blanket room (not visible) were saved. The mill was rebuilt using as much as possible of the Cotswold stone fabric.

72   The interior of the main block after the 1883 fire, showing the two cylindrical water wheels partially buried under huge piles of debris.

73 Early's fulling stocks in operation, possibly at New Mill during the 1890s.

74 New Mill, photographed from the south on 3 October 1972.

The Witney Volunteer Fire Brigade were on the scene within just six minutes, but their feeble hand pump could not stem the appalling destruction, 'the fire having got such a firm grip that the building resembled one vast furnace'. The firefighters therefore concentrated on saving a group of nearby cottages, together with the tucking shop and other outlying parts of the mill. After three hours, the fire was more or less under control, the main block having burned itself out. The cold light of a winter dawn revealed the extent of the damage, with expensive spinning machinery lying blackened and distorted among the smoking ruins.

On 20 January the *Witney Gazette* published an interesting plan of the mill at the time of its destruction, with the various departments clearly marked. There were around 24 different rooms or departments, including mule rooms, willey shops, carding rooms, spinning rooms, tucking shops, water wheels and an engine house. The machinery comprised fulling stocks, oscillating gigs, carding machines, spinning mules, scribbling machines and a hydro-extractor.

New Mill was reconstructed after the fire, and the opportunity was taken to re-equip the premises as a carding and spinning plant. Despite the severity of the blaze, some of the earlier structure was incorporated into the new building, and fragments of the main block, together with some of the outbuildings at the rear, predate the 1883 fire. In contrast, the northern end of the building has its windows at a slightly higher level, and this portion can be dated to around 1890; the architect was William Cantwell, who designed several other buildings around the town.

In its final, post-fire, configuration, New Mill was a relatively large two-storey structure, with ample fenestration and a low-pitched gable roof. The water wheels were retained in the modernised mill, water power being entirely free whereas the use of steam power incurred fuel costs. The water wheels were both 14ft long and about 10ft in diameter; a weir at the side of the mill enabled water levels in the head race to be adjusted in relation to seasonal fluctuations. The mill was the focal point of a small industrial colony, a foreman's house and about eight stone cottages being clustered around the main mill buildings.

New Mill was brought under the sole control of Charles Early and Co. after the 1883 fire, Walter and Thomas Early having withdrawn from the business; curiously, both of these brothers committed suicide, Walter Early deciding to drown himself in a water butt while, according to family tradition, 'Mad Tom' Early shot himself (his death certificate records 'General paralysis'). The mill remained in full use until the 1950s, when Earlys concentrated their entire spinning operations in a new department at Witney Mill. Thereafter, New Mill fell into disuse, and the site was finally relinquished in the following decade.

Witney Mill
Moving downstream from New Mill we come to Witney Mill, which was built on the site of one of the mills mentioned in Domesday Book. It was recorded as a fulling mill

76 *Witney Mill seen from Mill Street, showing the cylindrical brick chimney stack, dating from 1895. The angular block on the extreme left was built in 1934, while the gabled buildings on the right of the picture are dated 1905; the former house in the centre is probably from c.1750.*

75 *Witney Mill after the fire on 22 March 1905. The damaged structures were soon rebuilt, albeit with just two storeys, many of the quoins and other ashlar components being re-used.*

78   *The interior of Witney Mill weaving shed during the 1960s. The noise level in large weaving sheds was literally deafening, and many weavers suffered from hearing loss.*

77   *The buildings at Witney Mill were laid out on each side of the Windrush, necessitating a number of bridges across the head-race.*

79   *Lengths of blanket being stretched on the wooden tenter racks at Witney Mill, c.1890s.*

80   *Brand new Lancashire boilers en route to Witney Mill, being delivered to Witney station in 1896. Daniel Young was a local engineer and millwright, based in Bridge Street, who specialised in mill work.*

in 1277, though in those distant times the site was known as Woodford or (according to Dr Giles) 'Waterford Mill'. The oldest building now extant dates from around 1820, while the attractive range of two-storey buildings adjacent to the road were erected by William Cantwell in 1888 and rebuilt after a fire in 1905. The tall brick chimney stack dates from 1895.

A major fire that took place at Witney Mill on the evening of 22 March 1905 was as severe as the one at New Mill some 22 years before. At 5.15 p.m., just as people were sitting down to their evening meals, prolonged blowing of the factory's steam whistle raised the

81 *The Witney Volunteer Fire Brigade, which was formed by Herbert Smith in 1875 after a fire in Smith's mill.*

alarm, and Captain Smith and the Volunteer Fire Brigade were soon on the scene. Nothing could be done to save the main block, which was a three-storey stone building some 180ft in length, containing gigs, whipping and spinning equipment. Instead, the firemen directed jets of water onto some steel doors which connected the burning departments to the engine house and fulling block.

At 5.35 p.m. a powerful steam pump was despatched from Oxford, and members of a volunteer ambulance brigade set off on bicycles. Meanwhile, floors and expensive machinery crashed through the doomed building, while at the height of the blaze the red glow over Witney could be seen as far away as Reading. Vast crowds hindered the firemen in Mill Street, but as the fire burned itself out, the danger to the vital engine house subsided. Although the flames breached the fire doors at one point, a steady supply of water was available from the mill stream and the power plant was saved.

The damaged portion of the mill was subsequently rebuilt in a similar architectural style, the opportunity being taken to extend the façade along Mill Street and provide further accommodation between Mill Street and the tail race. The result was a jumbled accretion of buildings with a series of gable roofs; the engine house and boiler house were immediately to the left of the mill entrance, while extensive red brick weaving sheds extended westwards along the southern side of the head race. Further buildings, of stone construction, were laid out on a parallel alignment on the opposite side of the mill stream, bridges being provided as physical links between these two groups of buildings.

Witney Mill eventually extended over both sides of Mill Street, with a large red brick building with a ridge-and-furrow roof being erected on the south side of the road during the 1930s to accommodate spinning equipment and other facilities. Further expansion after the Second World War resulted in the provision of an enormous new factory to the west of the Victorian mill, and this uncompromisingly modern building eventually superseded most of the older accommodation.

82 *Bridge Street, prior to the construction of Bridge Street Mill, as shown on the Witney Tithe Map of 1839-40. William Smith's 'steam mill' extended over several of the properties shown on the Tithe Map, including plots 766 ('The White Hart') and the various closes and gardens between plots 763 and 753.*

83 *A striking view of Bridge Street Mill from the south bank of the River Windrush, c.1968. The ornate triple-arched façade was erected towards the end of the Victorian era. Note the square chimney stack, which was similar to that at New Mill, and the bridge dated 1925.*

84 *The main façade of Bridge Street Mill, looking north towards the High Street.*

Bridge Street Mill

The firm of Smiths Blankets was founded in the mid-19th century by William Smith (1815-75), who had started his career as a quill-winder at the age of eight. Hard work, and his own natural abilities as an entrepreneur, enabled this archetypal Victorian self-made man to start his own firm, and by the 1850s Smiths Blankets had acquired the first steam engine in Witney. The cost of transporting coal from Eynsham or Newbridge impeded further progress until the following decade but, following the opening of the Witney Railway in 1861, William Smith was able to erect Witney's first purpose-built 'Steam Mill' on a new site in Bridge Street. The new factory started production in 1866.

85   *Bridge Street Mill and Witney Bridge, photographed from Mill Street around 1899. The mill buildings are hidden behind a row of decrepit stone cottages and Witney's first National School – the later structure being distinguished by a tall Gothic-style window. The pre-1925 triple-arched bridge can also be seen.*

In 1840 the site of the mill consisted of several parcels of land in the possession of John Hollis, John Francis and others, and occupied by several tenants. These diverse properties comprised houses, gardens, stables, outbuildings and Witney's first National School, together with a large field or close at the rear of the various properties. As first constructed, Bridge Street Mill was partially-hidden behind these older buildings, but the construction of a new façade, with triple Jacobean-style gables, transformed the appearance of the mill in a most attractive way.

Bridge Street Mill was far bigger than it appeared to be, the long ranges of mainly Cotswold stone buildings that extended south-eastwards from Bridge Street having a length of around 280 feet. The entrance boasted an ornate glass and iron roof, while the square chimney stack proclaimed that the mill was steam operated from a relatively early date (later chimneys were usually cylindrical brick structures). The boiler house and engine were sited near the mill entrance, power being transmitted to various parts of the mill by means of shafting and belt drives. Little has been published on Witney mill engines, though former workers still

86   *Female weavers at Bridge Street Mill during the early 1930s; (left-to-right) Kathleen Keen, Vera Green, Violet Keen (née Cox) and Phyllis Keen.*

remember seeing the great horizontal compound engine in action through the windows or open doors of the engine room. Made by Marshalls of Gainsborough, the engine survived until the introduction of electric drives in 1945.

Mount Mill

Mount Mill, a mile downstream from Bridge Street Mill, was the home of James Marriott and Sons. The Marriotts were a long-established blanket-making family, though by the mid-19th century they were trading as farmers, coal merchants and dyers. At the end of the Victorian period James Marriott (1827-1904) decided to form a new textile company, and in 1897 work commenced on a new blanket mill at Mount Farm, near the site of the old manor house. The mill was designed by J. Kirk and Sons of Dewsbury, Yorkshire, and it opened for business in 1901 – although blanket production had apparently begun as early as December 1900.

87 *Part of Mount Mill, shortly after closure, looking towards the boiler house.*

Weaving had, for many years, been carried out on handlooms, which were fitted into odd corners of the mills or dispersed around the town in smaller workshops and factories. Mount Mill, in contrast, was planned and laid out for power weaving, and in this respect it was unlike the earlier Witney mills, which had originated as water-powered spinning or fulling establishments. The mill site was dominated by a large red brick weaving shed with a typical 'Northlight' pattern ridge-and-furrow roof; this large unobstructed area contained about a hundred power looms.

Spinning and other related processes were not, however, neglected, and Mount Mill included separate departments for carding, spinning and warping. Power was supplied from an engine-house on the south side of the weaving sheds, the boiler house having a cylindrical brick chimney resembling its counterpart at Witney Mill. The main departments were surrounded by other facilities, including a red brick storage shed on the west side of the complex; this was arranged on a parallel alignment to the neighbouring GWR goods yard, and it incorporated a small loading bay so that goods could be loaded or unloaded directly into waiting railway vehicles.

Before leaving Mount Mill, it is interesting to recall that this mill was equipped with a distinctive deep-throated hooter, which was blown at the start and finish of shifts. It was noticeable that when the Witney mill whistles were sounded for this purpose, they were never properly synchronised, with the result that the cacophony would sometimes continue for several seconds.

Farm Mill

Farm Mill, which was situated in Farm Mill Lane, occupied the site of the much earlier Walleys Mill. It was a typical three-storey water mill, built across the mill stream in the usual way. The 1899 Ordnance Survey 25in-map reveals that the structure was, at that time, an L-shaped building, with an extension on the west side of the main three-story block and a projecting wing at the rear, the latter part of the building being parallel to the head race.

88 *Farm Mill had ceased operation by the 1950s, and when this photograph was taken, some twenty years later, it was being used as an archival repository by Oxfordshire County Council.*

The main block, of Cotswold stone construction with ashlar quoins and dressings, measured approximately 76ft by 29ft at ground level. The window apertures featured slightly arched heads, those on the second floor being square, whereas the ground- and first-floor windows were oblong. The main block was certainly in existence in 1840, when it was shown on the Witney tithe map. In 1852, Farm Mill was being used as a blanket mill by Edward Early, though it later became a corn mill; by 1916 the occupants were Messrs Walker and Atkinson, corn millers.

Corn Street Blanket Factory

The Colliers were one of Witney's oldest blanket-making families. They were fully established in the Tudor period, and in later years they supplied large numbers of blankets to the Hudson's Bay Company. Their operations were, for many years, dispersed in small workshops and premises around the town, although they also owned a relatively large factory in a yard off Corn Street. This building had no power source and was strictly speaking a workshop for

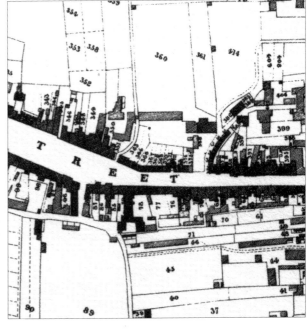

89 *An enlargement of the 1839–40 tithe map, showing properties 360, 361 and 362, which were owned and occupied by Horatio Collier. They comprised several plots of land, and incorporated a house, close, weaving shop, bleaching house, yard and gardens. The factory seems to have been connected to a neighbouring property by an archway or bridge which spanned Puck Lane.*

90 *A photograph taken c.1900, which shows the former Collier blanket factory in use as an agricultural machinery store.*

handlooms rather than a mill. The Corn Street factory was, nevertheless, one of the largest blanket-making establishments in the town during the early Victorian period.

The 1842 tithe map reveals that the property was then owned and occupied by Horatio Collier. It comprised several plots of land, and incorporated a house, close, weaving shop, bleaching-house, yard and gardens. The reference to bleaching is surprising, in view of the lack of an obvious water supply, and one must therefore assume that water for the bleaching process was obtained from wells on the site. The weaving shop was a three-storey Cotswold stone structure with serried ranks of rectangular windows and a gabled roof.

Colliers' ceased operations around 1878, and the former workshop then became Leigh's agricultural works and warehouse. From 1926 until 1928 it was used as a glove factory, following a fire at Pritchett and Webley's glove factory in Newland. In 1929 the property became the Swan Laundry, but this burned down in March 1937. However, the former blanket factory was soon rebuilt, part of the north wall being incorporated into an enlarged laundry building with a mansard roof and a tubular steel chimney.

Other Witney Factories at Woodgreen and Newland

In addition to the main mill sites, the Witney blanket manufacturers made use of a number of other sites, some of which were former handloom workshops, while others were purpose-built warehouses such as Earlys' premises in Newland. The Early family had weaving and warehouse accommodation in Newland in pre-industrial days, a substantial stone building being in place by 1820. In 1881 William Cantwell built a large three-storey warehouse and factory, an impressive structure of snecked stone construction,

91 *An interesting Seely sketch showing John Early's Woodgreen Factory in the early 19th century. A cross-wing was subsequently added at the north (left) end of the main three-storey structure, while the present building has a much lower roof pitch.*

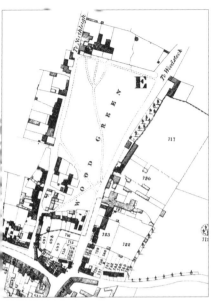

92   *The Woodgreen area, as shown on the 1839-40 Witney Tithe Map. John Early's property comprised plots 717 and 720, while property 723 was the Quaker Meeting House and burial ground.*

93   *The fire at Early's Newland Warehouse on 3 April 1975 did not cause irreparable damage to this substantial Victorian structure, although the building was nevertheless demolished shortly afterwards.*

94   *A Witney blanket label.*

A Genuine
Machine Washable
WITNEY MILLS
Acrylic Blanket
Made in Witney, England.

95   *Pritchett's three-storey 'Glove and Blanket Factory' in Newland was burned down on the night of 14 April 1926 and Pritchett's workers were relocated to the former Corn Street blanket factory while a new single-storey glove factory was built. Pritchetts never recovered from the fire, and the business was eventually liquidated, with the rebuilt glove factory being sold to Messrs Compton & Webb, uniform hat manufacturers.*

96 *Early's old factory building in West End which was, at one time, used for handloom weaving but later became a mop factory. This still extant three-storey structure is part of a complex of mainly 18th-century buildings, which were used as weaving shops by members of the Early family.*

with ashlar dressings and a slated roof; the gable end of the building was arranged at right angles to the street, and the window apertures had slightly arched heads.

The Woodgreen Blanket Factory was a three-storey Cotswold stone building on the east side of Woodgreen. The Witney Tithe Map of 1840 depicts a long range of buildings which, according to the tithe award, comprised a 'house, outbuildings, weaving shops, gardens and yard'. The property was owned and occupied by John Early (1801-76), the co-owner of New Mill and one of Witney's leading blanket manufacturers. A contemporary illustration suggests that the building was slightly taller than it is now, the roof having apparently been lowered at some time in the Victorian period.

As there was no source of water power the factory probably contained only handlooms – spinning and fulling being carried out by arrangement at New Mill or elsewhere. By the early 20th century the Woodgreen factory had passed into the hands of Charles William Early (1850-1943), but the building was no longer used for blanket-making and it finished its industrial life as a joinery. The former factory was eventually converted into flats by Charles William's daughter Janet.

A small factory situated in Newland, to the east of Earlys' warehouse, was shown as a 'Glove and Blanket Factory' on the 1899 Ordnance Survey map, although it was primarily a glove factory. This structure, a typical three-storey stone building belonging to William Pritchett, was burned down on the night of 14 April 1926. Pritchett's workers were relocated in Corn Street Mill, while a new single-storey brick factory was built in Newland. Although this factory was ready for operation within two years, Pritchetts never fully recovered from the fire and the business was eventually liquidated. The rebuilt glove factory was later sold to Messrs Compton and Webb, uniform hat manufacturers.

8

Victorian Developments

M id-Victorian Witney was a small, but busy town with a population of about 6,000. The 1841 census reveals that the parishes of Witney and Cogges contained 6,464 inhabitants, falling slightly to 6,251 by 1851 – the decrease in population being attributed to emigration. We are fortunate in that an excellent eye-witness description of mid-19th century Witney is given by the Reverend Doctor J.A. Giles:

> The town of Witney, which chiefly consists of two streets, one of which is about a mile in length, has a remarkably neat and cheerful appearance, and contains many well-built houses arranged with considerable regularity. The upper part of this fine street is called High-street, and the lower part Bridge-street. As the High-street draws towards the south it progressively expands, and in the broad area, is preserved an extent of green swards, through which is formed a wide and handsome gravel walk, leading to the northern door of the parish church. The church occupies the complete termination of the street, and forms a fine architectural finish to the general view.
>
> The town is within the jurisdiction of the magistrates of the county, and its internal affairs are regulated by two bailiffs, with constables and other officers. In a field near the church, is a house called the Mount House, which still retains traces of the walls with which it was once fortified. This house is said to occupy the site of an ancient castle of which little is known. Some antiquarians suppose it to have been the palace or manor house of the bishops of Winchester.

In physical terms, the limits of the Victorian town were still defined by Witney's medieval street layout, although by the 19th century there had been a considerable amount of infilling on the ancient burgage plots, some of which had become packed with small dwellings. Cresswell's Yard in the High Street, for example, contained a row of four two-storey cottages and a larger detached house, while Lowell Place, on the north side of Corn Street, was filled with rows of two-storey cottages. These yards and alley-ways were known locally as 'tewries'.

97 *A c.1900 view of Witney High Street, looking south towards 'The Hill'.*

Local Government in Victorian Times

The borough court, which had governed the town during the Tudor period, declined in importance after the 1650s, and at the start of the 19th century local government in Witney was exercised by the vestry. Originally a body of parishioners who met to determine the local church rate, the vestry wielded considerable power, as it appointed local officials such as the churchwardens, surveyors of highways and overseers of the poor.

A point which might be made concerning the vestry is that, although nonconformists were not specifically excluded, it was a primarily an Anglican body. This anomaly was rectified in November 1863, when the townsmen of Witney elected a Local Board under the provisions of the Local Government Act 1858. The Board consisted of nine members including two blanket-makers, a banker, a surgeon and a solicitor. Continuing central government legislation increased the range of local government activity, and in response to this changed situation the Local Board was replaced by an Urban District Council in January 1895.

The first chairman of the UDC was James Marriott, a coal merchant and member of a famous blanket-making family; he had been chairman of the Local Board since 1891

98 *(Left) An old postcard view of Newland, looking west towards Bridge Street. The tall end-gable of Earlys' Newland Warehouse can be discerned in the distance.*

99 *(Right) Picturesque old houses on the north side of West End at the start of the 20th century.*

100 *(Left) An 1890s view of Samuel Lea's ironmongers shop on the west side of Market Square. The Angel inn can be seen to the left, while the Bull inn can be glimpsed at the rear of the carrier's cart. The entrance to Clinch's Eagle Brewery was sited to the left of the Bull.*

101 *(Right) An attractive scene, showing old houses and cottages on the north side of Oxford Hill, probably around 1900.*

102 *(Left) Corn Street, looking east towards Market Square during the late Victorian period.*

103 *(Right) West End, as depicted on the Witney tithe map of 1839-40. It will be noted that no owners or occupiers are shown on the north side of the street apart from property No. 693: a house, outbuildings, garden and yard belonging to blanket-maker Edward Early. The 'blank' plots were part of Hailey.*

104 *(Left) Another view of West End, the street which inspired the First World War song 'The Old-fashioned Town' (see p.93).*

105 *The famous Witney Buttercross, from a postcard of c.1912. The remains of the supposed market cross can be seen beneath the post-medieval roof covering. Could the 13 ancient pillars that support the roof have been taken from the Anglo-Norman Bishop's manor house?*

and served on the Urban District Council until his death in 1904. Although Witney had a town hall, the Local Board invariably met in the workhouse, while the UDC held its early meetings in the Corn Exchange (opened 1863), but later moved to a large Victorian house on Church Green.

Witney Union Workhouse

Poor relief was traditionally given either as 'outdoor' or 'indoor' relief. Indoor relief was given to paupers who were housed in a workhouse believed to have been situated in the High Street. The New Poor Law of 1834 rationalised this system by allowing parishes to form 'unions' to facilitate the construction of large workhouses, each union being administered by a board of guardians. Witney thereby became the centre of a Poor Law Union encompassing 32 parishes, an area of 108 square miles.

106 *The entrance to Witney Union Workhouse before demolition of the archway.*

107 *An extract from the Workhouse Register for the quarter ending 19 December 1840.*

Witney Workhouse, which was erected on 'Razor Hill' (now Tower Hill) to a design by George Wilkinson (1813-90) of Witney, was one of the first 'new workhouses' to be built. Construction was under way by the summer of 1835, the paupers themselves being pressed into service as quarry labourers, and the building was 'nearly roofed-in' by the following November.

The completed workhouse was a typical Wilkinson design, consisting of a polygonal central block with radiating wings that contained accommodation for up to 450 paupers. There was also a gatehouse and porter's lodge, stables and an administrative block, while a chapel was erected in 1860 to a design by George's brother, William Wilkinson (1819-1901). It is interesting to recall that the Wilkinsons were both prolific architects, William being responsible for much of Victorian north Oxford, while George designed numerous workhouses throughout England, Ireland and Wales, together with several Irish railway stations, including those at Sligo, Mullingar and Longford.

The new workhouse had 194 inmates in 1841, rising to 288 at the time of the 1851 census – an increase of 50 per cent. The full-time staff at that time comprised a master, matron, schoolmaster, schoolmistress, porter, cook and nurse – the master being Benjamin Ward, while his wife Mary Ann Ward served as matron.

New Churches and Chapels

Victorian Witney was sharply divided along religious lines, the blanket industry being dominated by Methodist mill-owners such as the Earlys and Smiths, whereas brewers, bankers and professional men such as the Batts, Clinches and Wilkinsons were predominantly Anglican. The nonconformists were at their very peak in 1851, and the 'religious census' carried out in March of that year revealed that nonconformists totalled roughly half the population of England.

The Witney Methodists were so full of confidence in the middle years of the 19th century that they decided to erect a much enlarged chapel to the west of their earlier chapel in the High Street. The foundation stone was laid on 28 May 1849 and, less than one year later, on 22 February 1850, the new place of worship was officially opened by the Rev. Jabez Bunting, who had inherited John Wesley's role as head of the Methodist Church.

108 *The Wesleyans became particularly strong in 19th-century Witney, and the Methodist Chapel in the High Street reflects their dominant position within the town. Designed by James Wilson of Bath, it was formally opened by the Rev. Jabez Bunting on 22 February 1850. The 1851 religious census suggests that there were around 600 Wesleyans in mid-Victorian Witney.*

Designed by James Wilson of Bath, the new chapel was a curiously attenuated structure with a steeply pitched gable roof and tall Gothic windows. The building was aligned in conventional fashion from east to west, with its main entrance in the western gable,

109 *A postcard view of Witney High Street, looking north towards Bridge Street around 1912, with the Wesleyan Chapel visible to the right.*

which featured prominent buttresses and a four-light Perpendicular-style window. The buttresses were adorned with slender pinnacles which further accentuated the height of the chapel, while two smaller windows on each side were single-light lancets. Internally, the chapel contained a large gallery extending around three sides of the building, while the roof was supported by elaborate hammer beams.

The medieval parish church was at that time sinking into disrepair, and this historic building was, moreover, poorly sited in relation to the town centre. Conscious that the Methodists were planning a new chapel at the very heart of the community, the Rev. Charles Jerram, rector of Witney, decided that the Church of England should strike back in a spirit of friendly rivalry. It was agreed that a chapel-of-ease would be constructed on Woodgreen, ostensibly for the benefit of people living at the north end of the town who would 'not have to walk the distance to the Parish Church'; instead, they would 'have a church brought to their doors', the site of the proposed church being much closer to the centre of population than the original parish church.

Land for the new church was provided by 'the Bishop of Winchester and the Duke of Marlborough', while the architect was Benjamin Ferrey, a pupil of Augustus Charles Pugin. Guided no doubt by the strongly held opinions of Charles Jerram, Benjamin Ferrey drew up the plans for a 12th-century-style building with characteristic 'Early English' lancet windows. In accordance with Pugin's teaching, the Gothic details of Holy Trinity Church would be based upon careful archaeological studies of genuine medieval architecture, the entire project being infused with 'a desire for historical and religious truth'.

The foundation stone was laid, with great ceremony, on Friday 5 May 1848, and thereafter rapid progress was made. The building was completed in just one year, its cost being met by a Parliamentary grant of £250 and public subscriptions. The rector of

110 *Holy Trinity Church, an Anglican chapel-of-ease on Woodgreen. The 1851 religious census records 300 worshippers for the morning service on 30 March, and 600 for the evening service.*

Witney had raised no less than £500 towards the new building, while other subscriptions included £50 from the Bishop of Winchester, £50 from Lord Macclesfield, £20 from Lord Churchill, £52 10s. from the Rev. S.J. Jerram (curate of Witney) and £20 from the Rev. Jasper Jerram of Chobham, Surrey.

The new church was consecrated on Wednesday 11 July 1849 by Samuel Wilberforce, the Bishop of Oxford. The event was celebrated in typical Victorian fashion, with speeches and the customary 'cold collation' in the Staple Hall, which was specially decorated with evergreens and flowers for the occasion. The bells of St Mary's parish church were rung at intervals throughout the day, and *Jackson's Oxford Journal* reported that the town was 'the centre of unusual bustle and excitement in consequence of the consecration of the new church'.

In addition to these new Anglican and Wesleyan places of worship, a new Primitive Methodist chapel was erected in Corn Street in 1869. As befitted this proletarian sect, the building was of relatively modest external appearance, its main façade being pierced by a central doorway with three-light Gothic windows on each side. A circular window, placed above the door, added a note of distinction to the frontage of the chapel, while a datestone graced the apex of the gable.

Education in Victorian Witney

The development of universal elementary education in the 19th century resulted in the establishment of both National (Anglican) and Wesleyan Schools, the National School being founded at a meeting held in the Blanket Hall on 15 May 1813. At that meeting it was agreed that a 'Society for Promoting the Instruction of the Poor' would be founded to cater for the educational needs of both Anglicans and nonconformists. This worthy aim was enshrined in the following resolution, which was passed at the meeting:

111 *A c.1900 view of Witney Grammar School. The left-hand cross-wing contained the headmaster's private quarters.*

> That, considering the peculiar circumstances of the population of Witney and its neighbourhood, the schools formed by this society shall be open on Sundays as well as other days, to poor children of all sects and denominations, who will conform to the rules of instruction therein established; that the children of churchmen shall regularly attend divine service in the parish church; and those of dissenters either at the parish church, or at some other legally authorized place of public worship.

A small school was subsequently opened in Bridge Street, while in 1836 a separate infants' school was established by the rector of Witney, the Rev. Charles Jerram, at his own expense. These two Anglican schools were subsequently merged to form St Mary's Church

112 A recent view of the 17th-century schoolhouse at Witney Grammar School, which is perhaps the finest secular building in Witney.

of England School on Church Green, which was housed in a picturesque Victorian Gothic building dating from around 1860. Further National Schools were opened in West End and in Corn Street, while other Anglican schools were provided in the High Street, Newland and Cogges – the last-mentioned schools having been established during the 18th century through the generosity of William Blake, wool-merchant and lord of the manor of Cogges.

Meanwhile, having rejected the idea of sharing the National Schools, the Methodists set up a separate school in 1851, making use of their old chapel in the High Street. By 1853, the Wesleyan School had 130 pupils, together with one master and two pupil-teachers. The school was much enlarged in the 1880s, by which time it had started to provide a commercially oriented syllabus, with an emphasis on scientific and vocational subjects.

113 An Edwardian photograph of the Wesleyan Chapel and the adjoining Wesleyan School. Significantly, most of the local mill owners were enthusiastic Methodists, and many mill workers were encouraged to become Wesleyans. Methodism is still strong in the Witney area.

114 *The Clinches were bankers and brewers who, in the late 1830s, demolished many old cottages in the area to the west of Church Green to make room for the 'Eagle brewery'. Completed around 1840, the brewery was an impressive four-storey building of red brick and Cotswold stone with a tall stone chimney stack*

Witney Grammar School, in contrast, continued to provide a more traditional form of education, while Holloway's 'Bluecoat School' on Narrow Hill was an endowed foundation catering for the sons of journeymen weavers. In 1901 it was merged with the grammar school which, for many years, had a 'Holloways House' in commemoration of John Holloway, the founder of the Bluecoat School.

Clinch's Eagle Brewery

It used to be said that Witney was famous for 'Beer, Blankets and Beauty'. In earlier years, brewing had been carried out on a small scale, and there were at least five maltsters in the town by 1811. In that year the Clinches, a prominent local banking family, purchased the *Marlborough Head* (later

115 *Clinch's malt house at the rear of the Eagle Brewery, looking east towards the brewing tower. This property is shown as a 'malt house, hovel and close' belonging to John Williams Clinch on the 1839–40 tithe map, a 'hovel' being a local word signifying an outhouse or shed.*

116 *(Above right) Bottle labels from Clinch's Eagle Brewery, including a Clinch's Light Ale label and a Patens 'Eagle Light Ale' label.*

117 *A Messrs Clinch & Co. invoice dated 3 July 1926.*

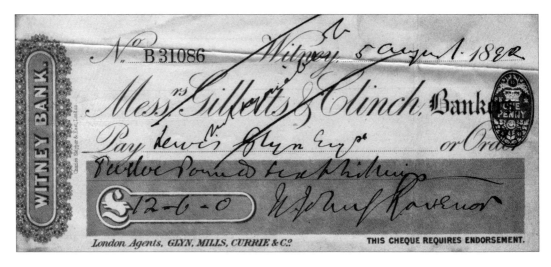

118 *A Messrs Gilletts & Clinch's cheque. The Clinches sold their controlling interest to Charles and Alfred Gillett of Banbury and Oxford during the 1870s, and the Witney bank then traded as 'Gillett & Clinch'. The bank was taken over by Barclays in 1919.*

the *Fleece*) on Church Green, Witney, and in the next few years they established a small brewery at the rear of the inn.

John Williams Clinch (1787-1871) assumed control of the family bank around 1828, while in the following decade John Williams and his brother James Clinch (1788-1867) established a much larger brewery on the west side of Church Green, many old cottages being demolished to make room for what became known as Clinch's 'Eagle brewery'. Completed around 1840, the brewery was an impressive four-storey building of red brick and Cotswold stone, with a tall stone chimney stack. In addition, the site included outhouses, stores, granaries and a large malthouse.

After the death of his brother, John Williams Clinch gained full control of the brewery but, following a row about the alleged 'misappropriation' of funds from the family bank, the brewing business passed into the hands of John Williams' sons. In 1883, William Clinch formed a new partnership with his son-in-laws Thomas William Foreshew and Bellingham Arthur Somerville (1853-1916), a district inspector in the Royal Irish Constabulary. On William Clinch's death in 1891 Clinch & Co. was formed as a limited company and thereafter the brewery went from strength to strength.

Like many other Victorian brewers, the Clinches played a leading role in local affairs, being promoters of the Witney railway and enthusiastic supporters of the 5th Oxfordshire Rifle Volunteer Corps – a volunteer military unit that eventually became part of the 2nd Volunteer Battalion, Oxfordshire Light Infantry. On a footnote, it is interesting to note that during the 1860s John W. Clinch, a member of the Clinch brewing dynasty, moved to Douglas on the Isle of Man, and set up another Clinch Brewery, which remained a flourishing concern for many years.

The Witney Axe Murder

Witney is not normally thought of as a setting for crimes of extreme violence, but in 1871 an axe murder took place in Meeting House Lane, the victim being a 33-year-old woman named Ann Merrick, who lived with her mother Esther Merrick in one of the stone cottages on the north side of the lane. There were two other occupants in the house on Sunday 30 July 1871; one of these was an elderly labourer called John Godfrey, while the other was a 36-year-old gardener called Edward Roberts, who was also known as Edward (or 'Ned') Robbins. The two men were lodgers, John Godfrey having lived with Mrs Merrick for a considerable time, whereas Edward Roberts had been lodging with the Merricks for a few months.

It appears that Edward had become obsessed with Ann Merrick, but she showed no interest in his advances. The couple seem to have been very different characters. Ned Roberts was a member of the lowest class of Victorian society, whereas the Merricks were what contemporaries would probably have described as 'the respectable poor'. Honest, industrious and hard-working, the Merricks were practising Christians, Esther Merrick in particular being a regular church-attender.

On the Saturday in question, Edward Roberts asked Ann if she would go to the *Marlborough* with him, but she refused. He therefore went out with a woman from a neighbouring cottage, and after a day drinking full-strength Clinch's beer, the burly gardener was soon blind drunk. Several people heard him shouting, swearing, and threatening to kill Ann Merrick. That night, however, he went quietly to bed, and the other occupants of the cottage assumed that all would be well on the following morning.

Sunday 30 July 1871 dawned peacefully enough in the Merrick household. As usual, Esther Merrick went to church, while Ann prepared Sunday lunch. At about 11 o'clock, the two lodgers were lazily sitting in the parlour smoking their pipes as Ann cleaned the floor. Suddenly, for no apparent reason, Edward Roberts went into the back kitchen, picked up a hatchet and then struck Ann Merrick twice on the head before returning the blood-covered implement to its usual place.

The innocent victim fell back onto her heels and assumed a kneeling position, her only words being 'Oh dear!'. Although conscious, she was gravely injured, the blows of the wood axe having inflicted a four-and-a-half-inch gash in the back of her skull and exposed her brain. John Godfrey, who had witnessed the attack, immediately called the neighbours to help plug the gaping wound in Ann's head.

119 *Terraced cottages in Marlborough Lane, originally called Meeting House Lane. It is believed that Ann Merrick lived with her mother in the centre of what was then a row of three cottages.*

Esther Merrick, having returned from church, was understandably appalled at the horror which confronted her when she walked through her front door, and she was led away from the house in a state of shock.

Charles Dorrington Batt, the well-known Witney surgeon, soon arrived on the scene. He found Ann Merrick surrounded by pools of blood, but still conscious, although a portion of her skull had been chopped off and 'only hung by a little skin'. Having replaced the bone, he bound up the wound, and attempted to make the victim feel a little more comfortable. In the meantime, Edward Roberts was walking along Marlborough Lane smoking his pipe, and when asked what he had been doing he replied, 'She served me bad and I hope she's dead.' He was taken into police custody and moved to Oxford Prison by train, while Doctor Batt did what little he could for Ann Merrick. Sadly, the unfortunate victim died some four weeks later on 25 August 1871, and Roberts found himself charged with wilful murder.

At the trial, which took place at Oxford Crown Court, there was some suggestion that the accused may have been guilty of manslaughter rather than murder, but his reckless comments about wishing to kill Ann Merrick were held against him, and the jury had no hesitation in finding the accused guilty as charged.

The execution took place at eight o'clock on the morning of Monday 18 March 1872 in the grounds of Oxford Prison. The prisoner had attended Divine Service on the previous Sunday, and eaten a 'hearty supper' of bread, beef and beer. He retired early, but was unable to sleep and had spent the early hours of 18 March reading the Bible. Dawn must have come all too quickly for Edward Roberts, but he managed to eat his breakfast of bread, butter and tea. This was followed by Holy Communion, after which the condemned man remained composed as he took his final walk to the scaffold.

The Bridge Street Shooting

In the early hours of 27 September 1884 William Smith, the proprietor of Bridge Street Mill, was walking round his premises, when he was surprised to see one of his men rushing about and inquiring where the shooting was coming from. He told him that it was a false alarm, but another man then ran up and said that John Rose 'was murdering his wife, and his son had shot him'. At that moment, 22-year-old John William Rose emerged from his father's house

120 *A c.1862 photograph of William Seely, auctioneer, artist, photographer and a founder member of the 5th Oxfordshire Volunteer Rifle Corps. William is wearing the uniform of a colour-sergeant, and his shooting trophies are proudly displayed. The 5th OVRC originally wore typical 'volunteer grey' uniforms with low 'shako' caps.*

121 *A detailed view of the Oxfordshire Rifle Volunteer shako badge, as worn by William Seely in the previous photograph. The badge, which is very similar to that of the Oxfordshire Militia, depicts an ox-and-ford motif within a crowned garter. The numeral '7' relates to the order of precedence of the county corps.*

122 *Men of the 2nd Volunteer Battalion, Oxfordshire Light Infantry, drawn up in Market Square around 1908. It is assumed that they have just returned from their annual summer camp. The 2nd Volunteer Battalion wore red tunics with white facings, in place of the earlier grey uniforms. The Corn Exchange can be seen to the left of the picture.*

and exclaimed, 'Father was murdering mother and I have shot him. Oh, where shall I get a doctor?' He was told that a doctor had been sent for, but that did not satisfy the young man, who rushed over the bridge to find a doctor. William Smith then went upstairs to see what was happening and found a man lying on the floor.

Having been arrested, John William Rose was charged with wilful murder, his father having died just 12 hours after the shooting. The prisoner told the police: 'I know I shot him; he was murdering mother. I shot once at the side to frighten him; he would not leave go, so I shot him.'

The case was heard at the Oxford Assizes before Mr Justice Lopes, and it was revealed that the deceased had 'lately taken to excessive drinking, and when intoxicated was extremely violent, and had on more than one occasion threatened to murder his wife'. On the night of the shooting, he had repeatedly abused his wife, and when he chased her and threatened to cut her throat with a knife his daughters had called out 'murder'. At that point the prisoner, fearing that his mother was in imminent danger, had fired two shots, one of which proved fatal.

Under cross-examination it was elicited that the deceased 'was a very powerful man indeed, and that the prisoner would have stood no chance in a hand-to-hand encounter'. The defence argued that the case was one of justifiable homicide, and the jury, 'after a few minutes consultation, acquitted the prisoner, a verdict which was received with great applause'.

9

The Twentieth Century

On 4 August 1914, following a period of growing international tension, the German army invaded neutral Belgium and Britain, having declared war on the aggressors, thereby became involved in a major European conflict.

The First World War

Many local men served in the Oxfordshire and Buckinghamshire Light Infantry which, since the army reforms of 1881 and the subsequent Haldane Reforms of 1908 , had been regarded as the 'county regiment'. At the start of the First World War the Oxon and Bucks. comprised five battalions, but the demand for manpower was so enormous that the regiment was expanded to thirteen. The regiment was involved in numerous actions on the Western Front, including the battles of Mons, Ypres, Loos, the Somme, Arras, Cambrai and Passchendaele. In addition, the much expanded regiment also saw action in Mesopotamia, the Balkans and in Italy.

In view of the prevailing anti-German feeling, a pub at 31 West End that had hitherto been known as *The King of Prussia* was hastily re-named *The Csar of Russia* but, following the execution of Tsar Nicholas II in 1917, the pub was dubbed *The House of Windsor*. On the subject of West End, it is interesting to recall that this street was associated with the First World War song 'The Old-fashioned Town', first sung in 1914. The writer of the song. Miss Ada Leonora Harris, used to stay in an 'Old-fashioned House' at 48 West End with her aunt and uncle – the 'Old-fashioned Pair' of the song. In its day, the 'Old-fashioned Town' was almost as popular as 'Pack Up Your Troubles' and 'It's a Long Way to Tipperary'.

The Witney mills were engaged in war production for the duration of the conflict, while Witney also became the site of a large Royal Flying Corps aerodrome, which was set up on 250 acres of requisitioned farmland at Downs Farm, immediately to the west of the town. Much of the construction work was undertaken by German

123 *(Right) Captain Archibald Grant, a former pupil of the Witney Grammar & Technical School, who died in France on 30th November 1917 while serving with the Essex Regiment. His parents lived in Gloucester Place.*

124 *(Above) Members of the Queens Own Oxfordshire Hussars, possibly in France, during the Second World War. Trooper Albert Horne (second from left) was killed in action on 16th November 1914.*

125 *A convoy of Army Service Corps vehicles on Church Green during the First World War. A column of men have apparently just arrived in Witney by train.*

126   *A captured German aircraft is displayed in the Market Square during War Bonds Week in March 1918.*

prisoners-of-war and Portuguese labourers, who were billeted in the workhouse on Tower Hill.

The airfield was opened in 1918 and from its inception was used for training pilots. The main aircraft movements commenced in March 1918, when Nos 8 and 24 Training Squadrons arrived from Netheravon. On 1 April the Royal Flying Corps was amalgamated with the Royal Naval Air Service to form the Royal Air Force

127   *An aerial view of Witney Aerodrome at the end of the First World War, looking eastwards. Seven large hangars can be clearly seen, with a row of canvas-covered Bessoneau hangars in the distance. The extensive domestic site, providing barrack accommodation, an officers' mess, a hospital and a guard room, etc., is visible in the foreground. The domestic site became an army camp during the Second World War, units stationed there being the Royal Engineers and the Royal Army Ordnance Corps.*

128 *A 1930s postcard view showing Church Green and Witney War Memorial.*

and thus, by the end of the war, Witney Aerodrome had become an RAF station.

The airfield occupied two sites, the hangars and landing area being on the east side of the road to Curbridge, while a large domestic site was situated immediately to the west. At its wartime peak the aerodrome boasted seven large hangars and, in addition, a line of eight canvas-covered Bessoneau hangars was erected to the west of the main hangar complex. As usual during the First World War, there were no properly surfaced runways, and take-off and landing operations were undertaken on a grass landing area. The domestic site included a whole range of accommodation, including a guard room, hospital, officers' mess and airmen's barracks.

The First World War ended on 11 November 1918, by which time the British Empire had lost around a million men, over 150 of these being from Witney or Cogges. Shortly before the end of the war, a War Memorial Committee had been set up with the aim of commemorating Witney's fallen heroes by erecting a cottage hospital. The committee hoped to raise £12,000, but the target figure was not reached and, as an alternative, it was decided that the Church Leys would be purchased from the Church of England for the sum of £1,027 2s., to be adapted for use as a public park and recreation ground. A granite tablet near the entrance to the churchyard, on the south side, records that:

> The Church Leys was purchased in 1920 as a public recreation ground out of funds subscribed by the inhabitants of Witney in memory of those who gave their lives in the Great War 1914-1918

Paths were laid out, ornamental trees and bushes planted, and bowling and putting greens were created, while some rudimentary children's swings, together with a massive seesaw and a chain maypole, also made their appearance at a total cost of £459 6s. 9d. The War Memorial, which was erected on Church Green and inscribed with 157 names, was dedicated at a well-attended service on 19 September 1920.

The Inter-War Years: New Factories
In 1930, James Walker and Co. of Mirfield in Yorkshire, one of the biggest blanket manufacturers in the country, decided to build a mill on a 'green field' site in The Crofts, thereby bringing new employment to Witney when other areas were suffering from the effects of the Great Depression. On 14 August 1931 the *Witney Gazette* announced that construction of the mill, which would initially employ 'one hundred hands', was

129 *Crofts Mill, photographed from the south, c.1980. The northlight pattern roof of the main weaving shed can be seen to the right, while the boiler house is visible to the left. Tenter racks can be seen in the foreground. The mill incorporated 5,250 square feet of floor space at the time of its opening in 1933.*

about to begin. Interestingly, it was stated that Walkers had purchased the Crofts site some ten years previously, but the underlying trade depression had hindered this ambitious project.

Crofts Mill was completed in the early part of 1933 at a cost of £19,000. The mill was essentially a large red brick weaving shed with a glazed 'northlight'-pattern roof, the main block being a single-storey structure measuring approximately 300ft by 110ft at ground level. There was a large basement, while peripheral buildings included the usual offices and store sheds, together with a boiler house and cylindrical brick chimney stack. In all, the mill incorporated 5,250 square yards of floor space.

Unfortunately, the opening of this new mill was overshadowed by a row over the rates. The local authority levied a rate of £770 per annum on the new premises, which Walkers argued was excessive in relation to the rates charged for other Witney mills. In support of their appeal, Walkers claimed that Crofts Mill differed from other mills in Witney in that it had no spinning department, all yarns being imported from their Yorkshire mills. The rates appeal was successful, and on 12 January 1934 the *Witney Gazette* reported that Walkers' rates bill had been reduced to £646 per annum.

130 *(Left) Crofts Mill chimney glimpsed across the roof-tops while under repair in 1978.*

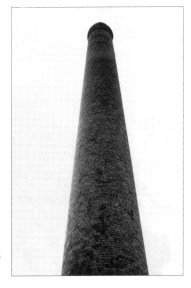

131 *(Right) A detailed view of Crofts Mill chimney.*

In 1921, Anthony Ernest Barrell, one of Witney's most successful businessmen, had built a large modern two-storey factory building on The Leys known as 'The Buttercross Works'. By the 1930s the factory was manufacturing mattresses, quilts and feather beds, as well as operating a large mail-order business which sold Witney blankets and offered a blanket-cleaning service. The Buttercross Works was destroyed by fire in 1939, rebuilt to a similar design, and then adapted for use as an aircraft components factory during the Second World War.

The Inter-War Years: Activities at Witney Aerodrome

132 *An aerial view of Witney Aerodrome during the 1930s. The foundations of demolished First World War hangars can be seen behind the surviving Belfast truss-roofed hangar. This structure, with its distinctive arced roof, measured approximately 174ft by 100ft at ground level. The hip-roofed building in the foreground was built in 1937 to serve as the headquarters of 'The Witney Aeronautical College'.*

Witney airfield was relinquished by the military authorities at the end of the First World War, and in August 1920 a *Times* correspondent lamented that this 'famous aerodrome' was being allowed to rot away, 'the canvas hanging in torn shreds from the wrecks of its hangars'. There were suggestions that the site might be utilised as a civil airport or as an 'air defence station' but, after due consideration, the Air Ministry concluded that Witney was unsuitable 'owing to the size of the aerodrome and the slope of the ground', which would involve 'unnecessary risk for pilots flying modern aircraft'.

Witney airfield nevertheless remained in use as a civilian flying school during the inter-war period, although all but one of its hangars was dismantled during the 1920s, leaving just one Belfast truss hangar *in situ*. It is interesting to note that timber and other material from the former RFC airfield was salvaged by Bartlett Brothers, the Witney building firm, and utilised for the construction of new semi-detached stone houses in Gloucester Place, Witney.

In 1939, a prototype aircraft of decidedly futuristic appearance was built at Witney to the design of Mr Percival Nesbitt Willoughby. Known as the *St Francis*, this unusual aeroplane was described at the time as a 'flying wing', although it might more accurately have been described as a twin-engined monoplane with a double-boom fuselage. The aeroplane flew for the first time in May 1939, and on 10 May *The Times* published an interesting description of a test flight that had taken place at Witney a few days previously, in which the 'all-wing aeroplane had taken off at about 60 mph and climbed steeply' before 'turning with a pronounced bank to come over the spire of Witney Church'. Sadly, just two months later, the *St Francis* crashed at Caulcott, near Bicester, killing the designer and test pilot.

The Second World War

On Sunday 3 September 1939, the United Kingdom found itself at war with Germany for the second time in less than twenty years. Ironically, the first year of the Second World War was so quiet that people spoke derisively of a 'Phoney War'. However, the sudden and unexpected collapse of France in the summer of 1940 heralded a more serious phase of the war in which, for the first time since 1805, Britain prepared itself for a possible invasion by hostile forces.

West Oxfordshire was thought to be relatively safe from German bombing, and for this reason large numbers of children were evacuated there from London on special trains at the start of the conflict. Later, in May 1940, soldiers who had escaped from Dunkirk were brought to Witney. In 1941, the engineering firm of Crawford Colletts Ltd moved from London to Witney and set up machinery for the production of colletts in the former workhouse, which was thereby transformed into a wartime factory.

On the night of 21-2 November 1940 Witney was hit by two high-explosive bombs, one of which landed on Church Green while the other exploded behind the Eagle Brewery. The Church Green bomb caused blast damage to the glazed roof of the weaving shed at nearby Mount Mill. Falling glass severed the warps in many places, and Marriott's workers were sent home for the morning while the 'chains' of warp were replaced. Other raids took place on local aerodromes, including a very damaging attack on RAF Brize Norton on 16 August 1940.

As the allied war effort got into full stride, West Oxfordshire became involved with preparations for the invasion of Europe. The Witney area was intimately connected with

133 *Evacuees from the West Ham area, photographed outside Witney Rectory in 1939, when Kathleen Jenkins was visiting her son Stanley Edgar Jenkins (second from right). The picture also shows Mortimer C. Jenkins, who was later stationed at Witney as an NCO in the Royal Army Ordnance Corps. Edgar Jenkins subsequently returned to the London area, and was killed in an air raid on Staines, aged 17, on 23 February 1944. His name was inscribed on Stanwell War Memorial.*

134 *(Left) Another aerial view of the aerodrome during the 1930s. The surviving First World War hangar can again be clearly seen, together with the former RFC domestic site, which became an army camp during the Second World War.*

135 *(Right) An aerial view of the aerodrome as it appeared shortly after the end of the Second World War. The two wartime Bellman hangars are prominent in the foreground, with the Belfast truss-roofed hangar to the rear.*

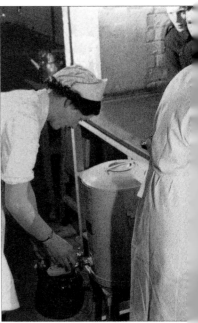

136 *Mr C.S. Thom (left), Wing-Commander Davidson (centre) and Flt Lieutenant Richard Jones (right) pose for the camera in front of a De Havilland Domine. Flt Lieutenant Jones, a former Battle of Britain pilot, was the only service test pilot at Witney.*

137 *A Second World War photograph of Witney Aerodrome showing airmen being served in the canteen.*

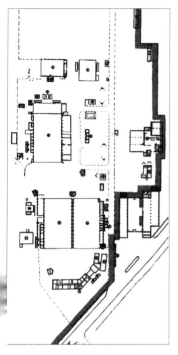

138 *(Left) A plan of Witney Aerodrome in the late 1940s, the Belfast truss-roof hangar (Hangar No. 1) and the conjoined Bolman hangars being clearly marked. The smaller hangars were of the 'Robin' type, and they measured approximately 75ft by 61ft at ground level.*

139 *(Right) The First-Aid room.*

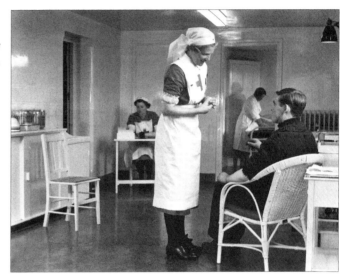

140 *A panoramic view of Witney Aerodrome, looking northwards from the roof of the Bellman hangars in 1943. The side of No. 1 Hangar can be seen to the left, with the 'panel shop' alongside and one of the small 'Robin' hangars in the centre background.*

141 *The Aerodrome's General Manager, Mr Philip Gordon-Marshall (third from left), carries out an inspection in No. 3 Hangars, accompanied by Nichi the Dog. A partially dismantled Hawker Hurricane can be seen to the right of the picture. Philip Gordon-Marshall was once described as a 'romantic, Richard Hanney-type character', with an uncanny resemblance to the Duke of Windsor.*

142 *A group photograph depicting some of the 700 civilian workers employed by De Havillands at Witney Aerodrome during the Second World War.*

143 *De Havillands workers attend a social gathering at Witney Aerodrome. John Dossett-Davies, who worked at the airfield as an aircraft inspector from 1943 until 1945, remembered the tremendous enthusiasm and* esprit de corps *which prevailed throughout the factory.*

144 *The entrance to the workhouse, which became an engineering factory when Crawford Colletts were evacuated from London to Witney during the Second World War.*

Airborne forces, local aerodromes such as Brize Norton and Kidlington being used for glider training. On 2 September 1942 a Miles Master aircraft hit the church steeple while towing a glider, bringing down the weathercock and crashing into a cedar of Lebanon tree in the rear garden of St Mary's Close at the entrance to Farm Mill Lane. Those aboard the aeroplane were killed, although the glider landed safely.

Witney Aerodrome had been commandeered by the Air Ministry at the start of the war and for a time it functioned as a much needed Relief Landing Ground for neighbouring RAF Brize Norton. In 1940, however, Witney was taken over by De Havillands as a Civilian Repair Unit, although test flying continued from the grass landing area. In its new role the airfield provided employment for over 1,200 people, planes being flown in for repair by female transport pilots, or brought onto the site in RAF transporter vehicles known as 'Queen Marys'. In all, the Civilian Repair Unit at Witney repaired over 700 Hurricanes and Spitfires, together with around 800 De Havilland aircraft, including Mosquitoes, Tiger Moths and Rapides.

The detached part of the airfield to the west of the main site became an army camp during the Second World War, the soldiers stationed there being members of the Royal Army Ordnance Corps, the Royal Engineers and other units. One of the RAOC detachments based at the Witney site was an Air Maintenance Company attached to the 6th Airborne Division flying from Broadwell or other local aerodromes.

At the end of the Second World War, the aerodrome consisted of a grassed landing strip, with a cluster of hangars and maintenance buildings at the northern corner of the site. No. 1 Hangar was the former First World War building, with its distinctive Belfast truss roof, while Nos 2 and 3 Hangars were standard Second World War steel-framed 'Bellman' structures. A much smaller building to the north of Hangar No. 1 was known as the Survey Hangar, while other buildings included a paint shop, battery shop, fitting shop, drawing office and canteen.

Religious Affairs

The most significant developments in the religious life of Witney during the 20th century were the demise of the Primitive Methodists and a revival of the Roman Catholics. The Primitives had flourished in Witney prior to the First World War, but in 1932 they were

145   *VE-Day celebrations taking place in the Market Square on 8 May 1945.*

amalgamated with the Wesleyans. The former Primitive Methodist chapel in Corn Street remained in use until the 1960s, when it was replaced by a brand-new Methodist chapel in Davenport Road. The Corn Street chapel was subsequently turned into a laundrette.

In 1738 Witney had contained just 'two small, poor families' of Catholics, the overwhelming success of the Protestant Reformation being such that Catholicism had largely ceased to exist in the West Oxfordshire area. A Catholic hierarchy was re-established in England by Pope Pius IX on 29 September 1850, and in the ensuing years there was a gradual revival of Catholicism, even in Witney. In 1916, a place of worship known as 'St Hugh's Oratory' was set up in a house at 1 Church Green, and masses were celebrated by a visiting priest from Oxford every fortnight.

As the Roman Catholic population in Witney slowly increased, it became necessary for the Church to procure a more suitable place of worship, and in 1933 a former National School building in West End was adapted for a new role as the Church of St Hugh of Lincoln. Although this single-storey Cotswold stone structure had not been designed as a church, like many Victorian Church schools, it was built in a Gothic architectural style that seemed entirely appropriate for a place of worship. This building was replaced in the early 1970s by the purpose-built Church of Our Lady and St Hugh at the bottom of Tower Hill. In 1948 Father John Roddy was appointed as Witney's first post-Reformation Roman Catholic priest.

Local Government in the 20th Century
Witney (with Cogges) had a population of 4,364 in 1901, to which we might add the 1,028 inhabitants of Hailey-cum-Crawley. The town had, since 8 January 1895, been

governed by an Urban District Council which carried out many improvements. In 1903, for example, the UDC completed a public water supply system, with a pumping station at Apley Barn and a water tower containing 80,000 gallons of water on Tower Hill (then known as Union Hill); 90,000 bricks were used in its construction, and the cost was £6,000. Sadly, the new water tower burst soon after its opening, flooding the surrounding area. Other local improvement schemes carried out under council auspices included the provision of a sewage pumping station in Dark Lane in 1902 and the construction of council houses such as those in Highworth Place, Moor Avenue and Park Road.

In 1974 the West Oxfordshire District Council was created under the provisions of the 1972 Local Government Act. In effect, the UDC and RDC were

146 *The water tower on Tower Hill, after the bursting of the tank.*

merged, leaving a few responsibilities in the hands of a town council of 12 members and a mayor, which now meets in the Town Hall. Meanwhile the church parish council, shorn of its former power, remained as a relic of the old vestry government, while the county council is responsible for highways, health, education and other important functions.

Educational Developments

Witney Grammar School had experienced a long period of decline during the 18th and 19th centuries, but there was a revival in the 20th century, and in 1902 the school was reconstituted as 'The Witney Grammar and Technical School'. Girls were first admitted in 1904, and by 1911 the school had around ninety pupils. In 1939 the school opted for county council control. In 1969 this historic school became a non selective comprehensive known as the Henry Box School.

In the meantime, the development of elementary education had received a major boost in 1930 with the opening of the Batt Church of England Central Secondary School in the spacious grounds of a large house in the High Street, which had been donated by the family of Charles Dorrington Batt (1828-1926). A range of classrooms was provided in a long single-storey school building, while Batt House itself was (in the 1930s) used for cookery lessons, woodwork and other activities.

These arrangements persisted until 1953, when the Batt School was amalgamated with the Wesleyan School to form a new secondary modern in Woodstock Road (now the Woodgreen Comprehensive School). As a result, the Batt buildings were vacated, thus prompting a reorganisation of Anglican educational facilities whereby St Mary's functioned as a Church of England Infants' School, while the old Batt premises became the Batt Church of England Junior School.

Further schools were opened in Witney as the town's population increased from around 6,000 in 1900 to 10,800 by the mid-1960s, and by 1972 there were nine schools within the town – the Henry Box School; Woodgreen Comprehensive School; the Batt School; St Mary's Infants' School; Blake C. of E. Primary School, Cogges; Hailey Road County Primary School; Our Lady of Lourdes Roman Catholic School; Tower Hill County Primary School; and The Queen's Dyke School.

The Demise of the Witney Blanket Industry.

In 1951, Witney became a centre of light engineering when Smiths Industries Ltd established a large factory on the site of the former aerodrome, which had been closed in 1949. By the 1960s this firm, which manufactured vehicle heaters and hydraulic equipment, was employing as many as 2,000 people, many of whom lived in the Windrush Valley Housing estate, which had been erected on part of the ancient deer park to the west of the town. The presence of Smiths and other industrial concerns such as Crawford Colletts ensured that Witney was no longer entirely dependent upon the woollen industry, although the town retained its pre-eminence as a centre of the blanket industry.

147 *The De Havilland factory at Witney was closed in 1949, and in September of that year the former aerodrome was sold to S. Smith & Sons (England) Ltd, who adapted the wartime facilities for use as an engineering factory, as shown in this c.1950 view.*

In the early 1950s, there were four Witney blanket-making firms: Earlys were well-established at New Mill and Witney Mill, while Smiths continued to operate from Crawley Mill and Bridge Street Mill; Marriotts remained active at Mount Mill and Worsham Mill, and James Walker & Co. were still operative at Crofts Mill. In addition, the Witney Blanket Company was still heavily involved with the mail-order business, while Compton & Webb was in full production at their Newland factory.

Mount Mill was badly damaged by fire on the night of 13 April 1953, when it became the setting for one of Witney's periodic factory fires. The fire was so serious that United States Air Force appliances were sent from nearby Brize Norton aerodrome but, fortunately, the damage was confined to the carding, spinning and warping sheds, and the weaving department was able to continue production using yarn from Marriott's other mill at Worsham, and from other companies.

In 1960 Marriotts were amalgamated with Earlys to form an enlarged undertaking known as Charles Early & Marriott (Witney) Ltd. Perhaps inevitably, it was decided that Witney Mill would became the main unit of production, and as a result Worsham Mill was closed in May 1965. The merger was, similarly, a mixed blessing as far as Mount Mill was concerned. It was agreed that conventional weaving would be concentrated at Witney Mill, but Mount Mill found a new role as a centre for a process known as 'Fiberweaving', whereby blankets were made without the normal

148 *New factory buildings take shape around the hangars. When completed, Smiths factory became Witney's largest employer.*

149 *A post-war view of the former aerodrome, showing the modern office buildings erected by Smiths Industries during the 1950s. At its peak, the Burford Road factory employed approximately 2,000 people – the run-down of the factory from 1988 onwards being a major blow to the town. In that same year, the Witney Foods Factory (formerly Brazil's) in Corn Street was closed, resulting in the loss of several hundred jobs.*

network of warp and weft. Two Fiberweavers replaced Mount Mill's 100 conventional looms, yet the combined output of blankets from Witney Mill and Mount Mill was increased by 50 per cent.

Messrs W. Smith and J.N. Philips was taken over by outside interests in 1967 and, after passing through several changes of ownership, Crawley and Bridge Street Mills were acquired by Moderna Ltd of Halifax. It was announced that blanket production would be increased from 450,000 to 720,000 per annum, but in the event the mills were closed in 1972 and 1975 respectively.

As the pace of rationalisation speeded up, Newland Warehouse was sold by Charles Early and Marriott Ltd to a property developer in 1973, and there were proposals to turn this handsome building into flats. In the event, planning permission was refused, but on 3 April 1975 the upper part of this fine Victorian building was damaged in a mysterious fire. Ten fire pumps attended the fire and the structure was saved from total destruction, but regrettably the damaged warehouse was later demolished to make way for residential development.

By the 1970s Crofts Mill was the last traditional weaving factory in Witney, Charles Early and Marriott Ltd having changed over to Fiberweavers and other modern equipment. Sadly, the mill was unable to survive in a competitive market, and it was closed in its entirety in May 1980 after a working life of just 47 years. The redundant factory was demolished shortly afterwards, and the site was then cleared to make way for a speculative housing development.

The demise of Crofts Mill meant that Earlys became the last blanket-making firm in Witney, remaining production facilities being concentrated at Witney Mill following the final closure of Mount Mill in 1975. Most of the Victorian buildings were disused, but the boiler house remained in commission to provide heating and hot water. Conversion to oil firing kept smoke emission from the 110ft brick chimney stack to a minimum, although occasional wisps of black smoke provided a nostalgic reminder of the steam era.

The trading name 'Earlys' was taken over by the Derbyshire-based firm of Quiltex early in 2002. Unfortunately, the District Council had granted planning permission for housing developments on the Witney Mill site, and Quiltex was therefore obliged to move its manufacturing operation away from Witney. This led to the official closure of the mill on 19 July 2002, and the end of blanket-making in Witney.

The Decline of Other Local Industries

Industrial decline was not confined to the blanket industry, other casualties being the Witney Blanket Company and Crawford Colletts factories, which were both closed in the 1980s. An even greater blow came in with the demise of the once-thriving Smiths factory on the Burford Road – the vehicle heater section being closed in 1988, while the Hydraulics Division succumbed in 2001. Compton's uniform clothing factory was also closed, although in this case the company – trading as CW Headdress Ltd – maintained a presence in the town by opening a much smaller unit at the Station Lane Industrial Estate.

The Witney Railway lost its passenger services under the notorious Marples-Beeching regime, and the last regular trains ran on Saturday 16 June 1962. Goods services ceased

150 *Early in 1965, the removal of the last section of rail on the abandoned route to Fairford made Witney 'the end of the line'.*

151 (Left) Station master John Barnby shakes hands with Mr J. Johnson, the driver of the last steam-hauled train to leave Witney, on 31 December 1965. The locomotive was a '61XX' class 2-6-2 'prairie tank'. The fireman (left) was Mr J. Compton.

152 (Right) The very last fare-paying passengers were carried on the Witney Railway on Saturday 31 October 1970, when a special excursion, the Witney Wanderer, ran from Paddington to Witney. Some 450 people made this sad final journey, which marked the official end of 109 years of railway history in Witney.

153 (Left) The Buttercross, viewed through the arches beneath Witney town hall, c.1930.

154 (Above) Witney recedes into the distance as the Witney Wanderer accelerates along the 'long straight line' beyond Witney Goods Junction – a view taken from the rear of the last train on 31 October 1970.

155 *(Left) Classical architecture in Witney: No.4 Market Square, visible in the centre of the picture and now Witney Post Office, dates from 1750. It has five bays and boasts a central Venetian window; once known as 'Hillrise' it served as a doctor's surgery until the 1960s.*

156 *(Right) An attractive scene, looking upstream from Witney Bridge around 1975. The flow of water at this point was constricted by the bridge aperture, resulting in the creation of a small 'beach' in front of the 17th-century house. In Victorian times, horses were able to drink from the river at this point.*

157 *(Left) Shops on The Hill, c.1968, including Margetts & Dyers' home decorating centre and Green's carpet shop.*

158 *(Right) Boots the Chemists, opposite the Post Office, was formerly the* Temperance Hotel. *An unusual building, which may date back to the 17th century, its shuttered windows have a distinctly French flavour. The* Cross Keys *inn can be seen to the right of the picture.*

159 *Domestic architecture on the west side of Church Green*

on 2 November 1970, and the very last fare-paying passengers were carried on Saturday 31 October 1970, when a special excursion train called 'The Witney Wanderer' ran from Paddington to Witney. Some 450 people made this sad final journey, which marked the end of 109 years of railway history in Witney.

The one success story, during this period of unrelenting decline, concerned the Eagle Brewery. Brewing in Witney had ceased in 1963 after Messrs Clinch and Co were taken over by the Courage combine, but the Eagle Brewery was used as a Courage distribution depot until 1978. Tragically – though it was once described as 'The best Victorian industrial building in Witney' – the main brewery building was subsequently destroyed to make room for the Eagle Industrial Estate. However, a micro-brewery was set up in one of the new industrial units and, after many vicissitudes, this new venture became 'The Wychwood Brewery'.

The brewery is now well established in the Eagle Maltings, at the western end of the former Clinch site, and in 2004, Brakspear's 'double-drop' brewing equipment was moved from Henley-on-Thames and installed in the Witney Brewery, which now brews Brakspear Bitter as well as Wychwood beers.

160 *(Centre picture) Clinch's malt house, in its present role as part of the Wychwood Brewery.*

161 *A final glimpse of St Mary's Church, which provides a tangible reminder of around 900 years of history.*

Select Bibliography

Ballard, A., *The Black Death in Witney*, Oxford Archaeological Society Report (1909)

Barratt, D.M. and Vaisey, D.G., *Oxfordshire: A Handbook for Students of Local History* (1973)

Bee, M., 'Clinch and Company, Brewers: an Oxfordshire Business History', *Oxfordshire Local History*, Vol. II, No. 2 (1985)

Beresford, M., 'The Six New Towns of the Bishops of Winchester 1200-55', *Medieval Archaeology*, Vol. III (1959)

Blair, John, *Anglo-Saxon Oxfordshire* (1994)

Bolton, James L., and Maslen, Marjorie M., *Calendar of the Court Books of the Borough of Witney 1538-1610*, Oxfordshire Record Society, Vol. LIV (1985)

Bond, C.J., 'The Origins of Witney', *Record of Witney*, Vol. I, Nos 3 and 4 (1978)

Cavell, Jane, 'Notes on the Monumental Inscriptions in St Mary's Church, Witney', *Record of Witney*, Vol. III, No. 6 (2003)

'The Witney and District in the Tudor and Stuart Period: Evidence from Probate Records', *Record of Witney*, Vol. III, No. 8 (2007)

'The Moulders of Witney: Soldiers and Publicans', *Bugle and Sabre No. I* (2007)

The Henry Box School: Its Place in History (2009)

Clements, Jeff, 'The Old Poor Law and the Workhouse in Witney', *Record of Witney*, Vol. III, No. 7 (2005)

Cooper, Trevor J., 'Aspects of the Old Poor Law in Witney 1536-1834', *Record of Witney*, Vol. I, No. 7

Cooper, N. and Morrison, K., 'The English and Welsh Workhouses of George Wilkinson', *The Georgian Group Journal*, Vol. XIV (2004)

Cross, D.A.E., 'The Industries of Witney', *The Journal of Industrial Archaeology*, Vol. I (1964)

Cunliffe-Jones, H., *History of Witney Congregational Church* (1935)

Davis, Peter, *Airfield Focus* (n/d)

'Royal Air Force Witney', *Record of Witney*, Vol. II, No. 3 (n/d)

Dossett-Davies, John, 'De Havillands, Witney 1939-45', *Record of Witney*, Vol. I, No. 11 (1981)

'The Leys, Witney – Portrait of an Oasis', *Record of Witney*, Vol. II, No.4 (n/d)

'De Havillands, Witney 1939-45', *Archive* No.39 (2003)

Durham, Brian, *Witney Palace: Excavations at Mount House, Witney* (1984)

Emery, Frank, *The Oxfordshire Landscape* (1974)

Fleming, Mary, *Witney Grammar School 1660-1960* (1960)

Gelling, M., *The Place-Names of Oxfordshire* (1953)

Giles, J.H., *A History of Witney* (1852)

Gott, Charles and Joan, *The Book of Witney* (1986)

Grundy, G.B., *Saxon Charters of Oxfordshire*, Oxfordshire Record Society, Vol. XV (1933)

Hall, H. (ed.), *The Pipe Roll of the Bishopric of Winchester 1208-09* (1903)

Hathaway, Mark, 'Witney Workless 1841 and 1851', *Record of Witney*, Vol. I, No.4 (1978)

Havinden, M.A., *Household and Farm Inventories in Oxfordshire*, Oxfordshire Record Society (1965)

Hyde, P., *The Oxfordshire Hundred Rolls of 1279*, Oxfordshire Record Society, Vol. XLVI (1968)

Hunter Blair, Peter, *An Introduction to Anglo-Saxon England* (1970)

Jenkins, Stanley C., 'Victorian Witney and its Railway' (unpublished University of Leicester MA dissertation, 1975)

    'The Industrial Archaeology of Witney', *Record of Witney*, Vol. I, No. 3 (1978)

    'The Great Fires of Witney', *Record of Witney*, Vol. I, No. 9 (1980)

    'Some Thoughts on the Topography of Saxon Witney', *Record of Witney*, Vol. I, No. 12 (1981)

    'The Witney Water Tower Scandals', *Record of Witney*, Vol. I, No. 12

    The Fairford Branch (1985)

    'Sir Charles Fox and Emma's Dyke', *Record of Witney*, Vol. II, No. 7 (1997)

    'Holy Trinity Church, Woodgreen', *Record of Witney*, Vol. II, No. 1 (1999)

    'Witney in the Early Medieval Period', *Record of Witney*, Vol. III, No. 2 (2000)

    'The Blanket Mills of Witney', *Archive*, No. 30 (2001)

    'Religion and Dissent in Witney', *Record of Witney*, Vol. III, No. 3 (2001)

    'Glimpses of Cromwellian Witney', *Record of Witney*, Vol. III, No. 7 (2005)

    'Witney and the 5th Oxfordshire Rifle Volunteers', *Bugle and Sabre No. I* (2007)

Lloyd Jukes, H.A., *Articles of Enquiry addressed to the Clery of the Diocese of Oxford 1738*, Oxfordshire Record Society (1957)

Monk, W.J., *History of Witney* (1894)

Plot, Robert, *Natural History of Oxfordshire* (1677)

Plummer, Alfred, *The Witney Blanket Industry* (1934)

Plummer, A. and Early, R., *The Blanket Makers* (1969)

Ransom, Phylis, *Round the Square in Witney* (1988)

Rodwell, Kirsty (ed.), *Historic Towns of Oxfordshire*, Oxfordshire Archaeological Unit (1975)

Roy, Ian (ed.), *The Royalist Ordnance Papers 1642-46*, Oxfordshire Record Society (two vols)

Sherwood, J. and Pevsner, N., *The Buildings of England: Oxfordshire* (1974)

Smith, Carmen, *Two Men's Ministries* (1983)

Weinstock, Maureen (ed.), *Oxfordshire Hearth Tax Returns 1665*, Oxfordshire Record Society (1940)

Wesley, John, *Journal of the Revd John Wesley* (eight vols, 1906-16)

Woodward, F., *Oxfordshire Parks* (Oxfordshire Museum Service, 1982)

Young, Arthur, *A General View of the Agriculture of Oxfordshire* (1809)

Index

Puck Lane, 13
Puritanism in Witney, 25-6, 29, 31, 32, 33

Quaker Meeting House, 39
Quakers in Witney, 39, 41
Queen Emma's Dyke, *see* Emma's Dyke
Queen's Dyke School, 107
Queen's Own Oxfordshire Hussars, *see* Oxfordshire Yeomanry

Radcot Bridge, Battle of, 11
Razor Hill, *see* Tower Hill
Reformation, the, 24, 25-6, 106
religious persecution, 25, 26, 27
Restoration, the, 37
Roberts, Edward, convicted murderer, 89-90
de Roches, Bishop Peter (*c*.1175-1238), 12, 16
Roman Catholic Church, the, 25-6, 27, 106
Roman occupation, the, 3-4
Rose, John William, acquitted of murder, 90, 91
Rowe, John (1626-77), Puritan minister, 33
Royal Air Force, 95-6, 103
Royal Army Ordnance Corps, 95, 99, 103
Royal Engineers, 103
Royal Flying Corps, 93, 95
Royal Irish Constabulary, 88
Rupert, Prince, 29

St Mary's School, 53-4, 85-6, 107
St Mary's Church, 13, 14, 17, 18, 26, 28, 35, 38, 48, 53, 113
Salisbury, 24
Seeley, William, artist and auctioneer, 14, 15, 20, 21, 22, 90
Shakenoak Roman Villa, 3, 4
Smith, William (1815-75), mill-owner, 61, 64, 73, 90, 92
Smiths Industries, 107, 110
Somerville, Bellingam Arthur (1853-1916), brewer, 88
Somme, Battle of the, 93
South Leigh, 54

stagecoach services, 46, 47, 50
Standlake, 2
Stanton Harcourt, 2
Staple Hall inn, 47, 85
Station Lane, 53
Strickland, Walter, Witney Railway Chairman, 51, 52, 54, 56
Swan Laundry, 76
Swinford Toll Bridge, 47

Taunton, 11, 16
Taylor, Thomas, house of, 20-1
Thames & Severn Canal, 47
Thames, river, 1, 3, 4, 7, 46, 47
Thompson, E.P., 42
Tower Hill, 18, 83, 95, 106
Tower Hill County Primary School, 107
Town Hall, the, 7, 33, 46, 82, 107, 111
trained bands, 21, 28, 29
Trelawney, Sir Jonathan (1650-1721), 38

Union Hill, *see* Tower Hill

vernacular architecture, 15, 19-22, 23, 24
Viking Wars, the, 6

Wadard, lord of the manor of Cogges, 9, 10
Walkers of Mirfield, 96-7, 108
Waller, General Sir William, 29, 30
Walley's Mill, 17, 75
wartime evacuees, 99
Waterford Mill, 70; *see also* Witney Mill
Waterloo, Battle of, 48
Welsh immigration, 15
Wenman family, wool merchants, 18, 19, 26
Wesley, John, 39, 41, 83
Wesleyan Chapels, 41, 42, 83-4, 86, 106
Wesleyan School, the, 85, 86, 107
West End National School, 86, 106
West End, 13, 23, 80, 81, 86, 93, 96, 106
West Midland Railway, 49, 53, 54
White Hart inn, the 25, 29, 30, 32-3, 72
Wilkinson, George (1813-90), architect, 83
Wilkinson, William (1819-1901), architect, 17, 83

William I, 9
Willoughby, Percival Nesbitt, aircraft designer, 98
Winchester, Bishops of, 6, 9, 10, 11, 12, 13, 16, 18, 19, 25, 31, 37, 84
Windrush Valley Housing Estate, 18, 107
Windrush, river 1, 5, 12, 13, 17, 21, 22, 63, 64, 66, 69, 70, 72, 73, 74, 75
Winterbourne Monkton, 39
Witney Aerodrome, 93, 95-6, 98, 100-3, 107, 108, 109
Witney Bridge, 21, 22, 25, 72, 73
Witney Deer Park, 18, 26, 107
Witney Feast, 14
Witney Grammar School, 24, 33-5, 85, 86, 87, 107
Witney Local Board, 80
Witney Manor House, 10, 11, 15, 19, 52
Witney Mill, 63, 64, 69-71, 108, 109, 110
Witney Railway, 50-4, 55, 56, 61, 73, 110, 111, 113
Witney Rectory (Trelawney House), 38, 99
Witney Rising, the, 26
Witney Union Workhouse, 82-3, 95, 103
Witney Urban District Council, 80, 82
Witney Vestry, 80
Witney War Memorial, 96
Witta's Island, 5, 13
Wolsey, Cardinal Thomas, 25
Wolvesey, 11
Woodford Mill, 13, 17, 69; *see also* Witney Mill
Woodgreen, 13, 18, 19, 23, 39, 76, 78, 84
Woodgreen Blanket Factory, 76, 78
Woodgreen School, 107
Woodstock, 30, 44, 47
Worcester, Battle of, 30
World Wars: First, 93-6; Second, 99-10
Worsham Mill, 63, 64, 108, 109
Wychwood Forest, 1, 5, 10
Wychwood Brewery, 113

Yarnton, 50, 51
Young, Arthur, 48
Ypres, Battle of, 93